T0207711

SEARCH

THE

SCRIPTURES

Bible Devotions and Puzzle Fun

MICHAEL E. LEONARD

WESTBOW
PRESS®
A DIVISION OF THOMAS NELSON
& ZONDERVAN

WestBow Press books may be ordered through booksellers or by contacting:

WestBow Press
A Division of Thomas Nelson & Zondervan
1663 Liberty Drive
Bloomington, IN 47403
www.westbowpress.com
844-714-3454

Unless otherwise indicated, all Scripture is taken from the King James Version of the Bible.

Scripture marked (NKJV) taken from the New King James Version®. Copyright © 1982 by Thomas Nelson. Used by permission. All rights reserved.

Scripture quotations marked (ESV) are from the ESV® Bible (The Holy Bible, English Standard Version®), copyright © 2001 by Crossway, a publishing ministry of Good News Publishers. Used by permission. All rights reserved.

Scripture quotations taken from the (NASB®) New American Standard Bible®, Copyright © 1960, 1971, 1977, 1995, 2020 by The Lockman Foundation. Used by permission. All rights reserved. www.lockman.org

ISBN: 978-1-6642-5221-9 (sc)
ISBN: 978-1-6642-5222-6 (hc)
ISBN: 978-1-6642-5220-2 (e)

Print information available on the last page.

WestBow Press rev. date: 12/15/2021

CONTENTS

NAMES OF THE LORD

The first three puzzles have to do with names or descriptions of God as revealed in scripture. There are many ways in which our wonderful Lord is described. Stop to read and quietly meditate on the following, and you will be blessed.

In Genesis, He is the Creator of heaven and earth.

In Exodus, He is the great I AM.

In Leviticus, He is the peace offering.

In Numbers, He is the Star out of Jacob.

In Deuteronomy, He is the great, mighty, awesome God.

In Joshua, He is the Captain of the Lord's host.

In Judges, He is the Lord God of Israel.

In Ruth, He is the Kinsman Redeemer.

In 1 Samuel, He is Lord of hosts, God of the armies of Israel.

In 2 Samuel, He is the Rock of my salvation.

In 1 Kings, He is the still, small voice.

In 2 Kings, He grants a double portion of His Spirit.

In 1 Chronicles, He is glory and victory and majesty.

In 2 Chronicles, He is a help in the battle.

In Ezra, He is the Lord, the God of heaven.

In Nehemiah, He is a God of forgiveness, gracious and compassionate, abounding in loving-kindness.

In Esther, He is relief and deliverance for the Jews.

In Job, He is the Lord who gives and takes away.

In Psalms, He is my Shepherd.

In Proverbs, He is counsel, wisdom, and understanding.

In Ecclesiastes, it is He who makes everything beautiful in His time.

In Song of Solomon, He is the Chief among ten thousand.

In Isaiah, He is wonderful, Counselor, mighty God, everlasting Father, and Prince of Peace.

In Jeremiah, He is the Balm of Gilead.

In Lamentations, He is the God whose compassion is new every morning.

In Ezekiel, He is a plant of renown.

In Daniel, He is the Ancient of Days.

In Hosea, it is He who reigns righteousness.

In Joel, He is the hope of His people.

In Amos, it is He who reveals His secret counsel to His prophets.

In Obadiah, He is the Lord of Justice.

In Jonah, He is the God of compassion.

In Micah, He is ruler in Israel.

In Nahum, He is a stronghold in the day of trouble.

In Habakkuk, He is the everlasting one.

In Zephaniah, He is a victorious warrior.

In Haggai, He is a Spirit abiding in our midst.

In Zechariah, He is the Branch.

In Malachi, He is the Sun of righteousness.

In Matthew, He is the Son of David.

In Mark, He is the Son of Man.

In Luke, He is the Light to the Gentiles.

In John, He is the Son of God.

In Acts, He is the Holy One and just.

In Romans, He is Lord over all.

In 1 Corinthians, He is the first fruits of those who slept.

In 2 Corinthians, He is the Unspeakable Gift.

In Galatians, He is the Spirit of His Son.

In Ephesians, He is head over all things.

In Philippians, He is a servant.

In Colossians, He is the image of the invisible God.

In 1 Thessalonians, He is His Son from heaven.

In 2 Thessalonians, He is the Lord of Peace.

In 1 Timothy, He is Mediator between God and man.

1n 2 Timothy, He is the Righteous Judge.

In Titus, He is the great God.

In Philemon, He is the Lord Jesus Christ.

In Hebrews, He is the Author and Finisher of our faith.

In James, He is that worthy name.

In 1 Peter, He is the Lamb without blemish or spot.

In 2 Peter, He is the Day Star.

In 1 John, He is the Advocate.

In 2 John, He is the Son of the Father.

In 3 John, He is the Name.

In Jude, He is Master and Lord.

In Revelation, He is King of kings and Lord of lords.

May you be encouraged as you seek the Lord. "Great is the Lord and greatly to be praised, and His greatness is unsearchable" (Psalm 145:3).

THE
CHARACTER
OF GOD

The more we know about God, the more we love Him and the more we desire to be like Him. Too many people have wrong conceptions about God. What does He have to say about himself? Meditate on God's character, as revealed in the Scriptures below. He always acts consistently with His character. He never changes.

Look up the given Scriptures references to answer the following about God.

I. God is ...

1. _____ 1 John 4:8
2. _____ 1 John 1:5
3. _____ Hebrews 12:29
4. _____ John 4:24
5. _____ John 1:1

II. God is described in nature as ...

6. _____ 1 Kings 8:27
7. _____ Psalm 90:2
8. _____ Jeremiah 32:17, 27
9. _____ Psalm 139: 7-10
10. _____ 1 John 3:20

III. Names of God include ...

11. _____ Genesis 14:18-22
12. _____ Genesis 15:2
13. _____ Genesis 28:3
14. _____ Exodus 3:14
15. _____ Isaiah 43:3
16. _____ Matthew 6:26

V. God loves . . .
    17. _____ John 15:9
    18. _____ John 3:16
V. God hates . . .
    19. _____

    _____ Proverbs 6:16-19
VI. God delights in . . .
    20. _____
    Jeremiah 9:24

"I AM"

Jesus Christ did more than merely walk the earth as a "good man" who did "good things." He means *much* more to us than that. As you work this puzzle, stop and consider these claims which Christ made about himself. How do they relate to you as you walk with Him?

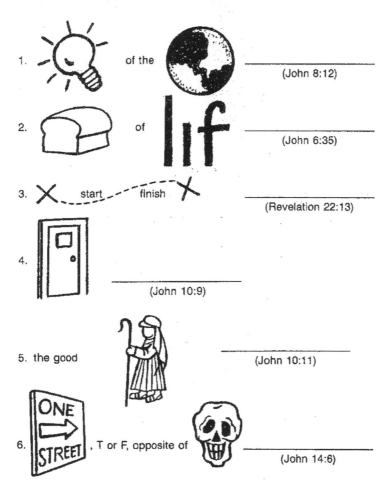

1.  of the  ____________________ (John 8:12)

2.  of lif ____________________ (John 6:35)

3. 

____________________ (Revelation 22:13)

4.  ____________________ (John 10:9)

5. the good  ____________________ (John 10:11)

6. 

, T or F, opposite of  ____________________ (John 14:6)

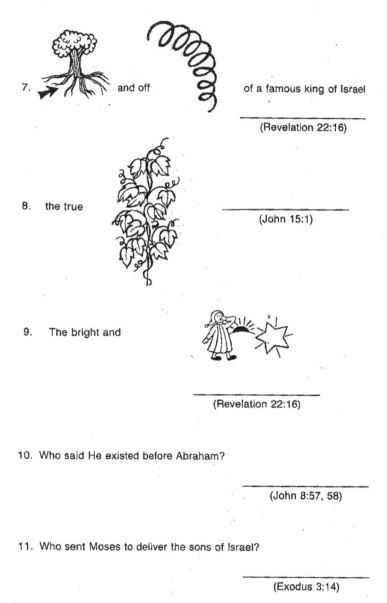

7.   and off   of a famous king of Israel

_____

(Revelation 22:16)

8.   the true

_____

(John 15:1)

9.   The bright and

_____

(Revelation 22:16)

10. Who said He existed before Abraham?

_____

(John 8:57, 58)

11. Who sent Moses to deliver the sons of Israel?

_____

(Exodus 3:14)

THE MANY NAMES OF CHRIST

Did you know that the Gospel of Matthew was written primarily to present Jesus Christ as the Jewish Messiah? That Mark directed his writing toward the Gentiles? That Luke emphasizes Jesus's humanity and John emphasizes His deity? That our Lord is described or alluded to in many fascinating ways throughout scripture? Read God's Word to discover just how wonderful Jesus really is!

Give the correct book of the Bible with which each of the following descriptions of Christ is best associated. (Notice how many Old Testament references are included.)

Genesis   Numbers   Joshua   Psalms   Song of Solomon   Isaiah
Jeremiah   Daniel   Malachi   Matthew   Luke   John
Hebrews   1 Peter   Revelation

1. Ancient of Days _____
2. Author and Finisher of our faith _____
3. Beginning and end _____
4. Branch of righteousness _____
5. Captain of the Lord's host _____
6. Chief Shepherd _____
7. King of Glory _____
8. Lamb of God _____
9. Prince of Peace _____
10. Rose of Sharon _____
11. Seed of the woman _____
12. Son of David _____
13. Son of Man _____
14. Star of Jacob _____
15. Sun of righteousness _____

THE EARLY EARTH

Many people, even some believers, question the accuracy of the first eleven chapters of the book of Genesis. Especially attacked is the story of the great flood during the time of Noah. Many believe that such a universal flood could not have occurred. However, Jesus refers to it when He speaks about His Second Coming (see Matthew 24:37–39). If our Lord confirms the great flood, we can be sure that it actually happened. Jesus also affirms God's creation of male and female in Mark 10:6.

In 2 Timothy, we are told that all scripture is inspired by God. And God never lies. From the creation to the incident at the Tower of Babel and beyond, you can believe that His Word is trustworthy and true.

ARK WORK

Of all the inhabitants of the earth at that time, only Noah "found grace in the eyes of the Lord" (Genesis 6:8). All those who did not perished. The Bible says in the future there will come yet another judgment of God upon the earth. Once again God will preserve those who are His, just as He did in the days of Noah. Are you safe aboard the "ark" today?

Complete the following crossword puzzle. All answers refer to Noah and the great flood. All Scriptures are in Genesis.

Across:
3. passengers on the ark (7:8, 9)
5. a son of Noah (5:32)
6. number of people saved (7:13)
8. wood covering (6:14)
10. covered the earth (7:20-22)
13. covenant of God (9:13)
14. shut the ark door (7:16)
16. leaf in the dove's mouth (8:11)

Down:
1. number of stories on the ark (6:16)
2. a son of Noah (5:32)
4. builder of the ark (6:13, 14)
7. type of wood used for the ark (6:14)
9. a son of Noah (5:32)
11. sent forth by Noah (8:7)
12. number of days and nights of rain (7:12)
15. sent forth by Noah (8:8)

11

ABRAHAM

Abraham was a man of great faith. According to Genesis 15:6, He believed God's promise of a multitude of descendants, and the Lord accounted it to him as righteousness. In Romans 4:18–21, we are told that despite his circumstances, he believed. He did not waver in unbelief but was strengthened in faith, giving glory to God.

Do you want to grow in faith? Romans 10:17 says that faith comes by hearing, and hearing by the Word of God. To grow in your faith, the best thing to do is read and meditate on biblical passages. You will come to know more about the Lord—how He acts, how He thinks, how He relates to you, and how to relate to Him. Read about heroes of faith in Hebrews chapter 11. Consider also such passages as Romans 4:13 through 5:2, Hebrews 4:2 and 6:12, James 2:17, and Ephesians 6:16. As time goes on, your faith will increase, and you too will give glory to God.

THE HALL OF FAITH

"Now faith is the substance of things hoped for, the evidence of things not seen" (Hebrews 11:1). The Lord desires each of us to develop strong faith, for this is what pleases Him. (See verse 6.) The men and women highlighted in this chapter were fallible human beings, just as we are. But their faith was commendable. We can learn from their example.

Listed below are some verses from Hebrews 11, as well as names of people of faith which appear in them. What they did by faith is "not yet seen." Decipher the code to determine it.

Code:			
A is B	H is G	O is P	U is V
B is A	I is J	P is O	V is U
C is D	J is I	Q is R	W is X
D is C	K is L	R is Q	X is W
E is F	L is K	S is T	Y is Z
F is E	M is N	T is S	Z is Y
G is H	N is M		

	Verse	Name	By Faith ...
1.	4	Abel	PEEFQFC B NPQF FWDFKKFMS TBDQJEJDF
			_____
2.	5	Enoch	OKFBTFC HPC
			_____
3.	7	Noah	OQFOBQFC BM BQL SP SGF TBUJMH
			_____
			PE GJT GPVTF
			_____

4. 11 Sarah CFKJUFQFC B DGJKC XGFM OBTS BHF

_____

5. 17 Abraham PEEFQFC VO JTBBD

_____

6. 20 Isaac AKFTTFC IBDPA BMC FTBV DPMDFQMJMH

_____

SGJMHT SP DPNF

_____

7. 21 Jacob AKFTTFC APSG TPMT PE IP-TFOG

_____

8. 22 Joseph HBUF DPNNBMCNFMS DPMDFQMJMH

_____

GJT APMFT

_____

9. 28 Moses LFOS SGF OBTTPUFQ

_____

10. 31 Rahab QFDFJUFC SGF TOJFT

_____

JACOB AND JOSEPH

When I was a young boy, my father was a railroad inspector who worked at various ports of entry. His job was to determine the amount and cause of any damage done to cargo transported by rail. This usually saved the railroad money. He once spent a period of time working at a fruit mart. I remember him bringing home samples of some of the largest, most delicious fruit you could possibly imagine. Such luscious fruit is not seen in grocery stores because expensive gourmet restaurants buy it all up. I remember the time I promised my teacher I would bring her a gift. What she received was by far the biggest red apple she had ever seen. She and my classmates were amazed.

When the patriarch Jacob left his father and mother to escape the wrath of his brother, Esau, he possessed nothing except his staff. Years later, upon his return, he was a rich man who owned many flocks and herds, along with wives and children (Genesis 32:1–10). When Joseph was sold as a slave by his brothers, he had nothing. Seventeen years later, despite being enslaved and falsely imprisoned, he was promoted to second in command of the entire land of Egypt (Genesis 41:38–41).

My teacher received much more than she expected. Jacob and Joseph had no idea how much God had in store for them. There are times when the Lord may wish to bless us in ways far beyond our expectations. Let us remain faithful to Him. Read Ephesians 3:20. God is able to do more than we could ever ask or think.

JOSEPH:
UP FROM THE DEPTHS

Joseph is one of the few men in the Bible of whom virtually nothing negative is said. He was a remarkable man who endured injustice and mistreatment without denying God. He knew the Lord was in control of all his circumstances. In due time, God exalted him as a result of his faith. We can learn much from Joseph's example.

Answer the following, all of which refer to the life of Joseph. To fill in the answers, you must work "up" each time. All the answers are found in Genesis.

Clues:
1. Joseph's father (37:2)
2. Joseph's father-in-law was priest of (41:45)
3. a special gift to Joseph from his father (37:3)
4. held as ransom when the brothers of Joseph returned to their own land during the famine (42:24-26)
5. Joseph's wife (Genesis 41:45)
6. one of Joseph's sons (41:50, 52)
7. Joseph's younger brother (43:14)
8. Joseph's master when he was a slave (39:1, 2)
9. country Joseph was made prime minister over (41:41)
10. because of them Joseph angered his brothers (37:5-11)
11. Joseph's people (40:15)
12. Joseph's mother (30:22-24)
13. where Joseph was sent after falsely accused by his master's wife (39:20)
14. had a dream interpreted by Joseph while in prison (40:16-19)
15. seen in Pharaoh's dream (41:22-24)

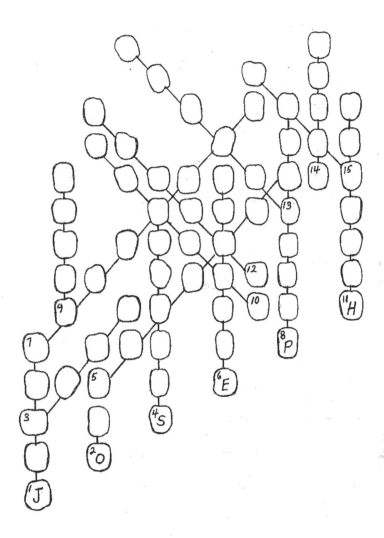

MOSES

One complaint often heard from unbelievers is "If God exists, why don't we see Him? Why does He hide Himself?" Ignoring nature and all the evidence of creation surrounding them (Romans 1:20), they flippantly demand some kind of supernatural appearance by God before they will believe in Him.

Such people should read about Moses and the Israelites during the time of the Exodus. After the Lord gave the Ten Commandments to Moses atop Mount Sinai, the people witnessed thunder, lightning flashes, and trumpet sounds. They were so afraid that they said they wanted only Moses to speak to them, not God directly, lest they die (Exodus 20:18–21). Later, when Moses himself asked the Lord to show him His glory, God had to put him in the cleft of a rock, covering him with His hand. God only let Moses see His back as His glory passed by, stating, "You cannot see My face, for no man shall see My face and live" (see Exodus 33:17–23 NKJV).

At present, we cannot stand before God's holiness. However, once in heaven, believers who have accepted Jesus as their Savior will someday be able to see Him (Revelation 22:3–4) and live with Him forever.

THE TEN PLAGUES

Just as surely as God is a God of love, He is also a just God who does not overlook sin. The Lord heard the cries of His people who had been in bondage for hundreds of years. So He delivered them from the Egyptians through a series of terrible plagues. God's nature does not change, and He still vindicates His people today. Only remember, He is the one who judges (Romans 12:19), not you!

In order to solve this puzzle, (1) use the given clues to identify the plagues, (2) arrange the plagues by number in order from first to last (1 = the first plague, 2 = the second plague, etc.), (3) write out the accompanying letters of the alphabet in this same order so you can spell out who allowed them to come to pass! (All these clues are in the book of Exodus.)

Clue	Plague	Order
1. painful sores—R (9:8-12)	_____	_____
2. wins the jumping contest—H (8:1-15)	_____	_____
3. thunder accompanies this—D (9:18-24)	_____	_____

4. can't see—
   (10:21-23)   _____ _____

5. red in color—T
   (7:20-25)   _____ _____

6. like a grasshopper—G
   (10:1-20)   _____ _____

7. milk and meat
   shortage—O
   (9:1-7)   _____ _____

8. attracted to rubbish
   heaps—L
   (8:20-24)   _____ _____

9. skull and crossbones—
   D (12:29, 30)   _____ _____

10. small and very
    bothersome—E
    (8:16-19)   _____ _____

Letters spell out: _____

JOSHUA

If you look about, you will notice that through many books, videos, seminars, speaking engagements, the internet, and other means, people claim to reveal (in one area or another) how to be successful. Resources such as these are very popular because everyone wants to succeed and prosper.

Joshua 1:8 reveals God's recipe for success. Upon the death of Moses, it was up to Joshua to lead the Israelites into the land that God had promised them. There would be many obstacles ahead. The Lord promised Joshua that he would succeed, but only if he meditated on the Law of Moses and did all it commanded.

How often do we spend quality time meditating on God's Word? Time goes by ever so quickly, and much of what we do is of little or no value in light of eternity. I regret how much time I've wasted in the past—time that can never be recovered. Of course, spending time in scripture does little good if we fail to put into practice what we are reading. It is a matter of choice.

Do you wish for true success in your life? Joshua was not perfect. He made mistakes. But he and his house vowed to serve the Lord (24:15). He chose God's way of success, and so can you.

TOTAL OBEDIENCE

All sorts of people profess to "love the Lord." But what is prime evidence of such love? Jesus declares in John 14:15, "If ye love me, keep my commandments." God wants us to obey Him not because He wants to dampen our pleasure, but because he loves us and knows what is best for us at all times. Obedience to God is essential if we desire loving fellowship with Him.

Fill in the answers in this puzzle. All refer to positive examples of individuals who obeyed the Lord. Clues are as follows:

1. He boldly told the Jewish council, "We ought to obey God rather than men" (Acts 5:27-29).
2. He built the ark according to God's command (Genesis 6:13-22).
3. He left his tax office and followed at Jesus' command (Matthew 9:9).
4. He answered the Lord's call by declaring, "Here am I; send me" (Isaiah 6:1-8).
5. He told King Agrippa, "I was not disobedient unto the heavenly vision" (Acts 26:1, 19).
6. He exhorted the Israelites by declaring, "Choose you this day whom ye will serve ... but as for me and my house, we will serve the Lord" (Joshua 24:2, 15).
7. He obeyed God by departing his homeland and traveling to an unknown land (Genesis 12:1-4).
8. He did not depart from following the Lord; there was no other king of Judah like him in this respect (2 Kings 18:1-6).

9. He inquired of the Lord, then obeyed Him by capturing Hebron. He was then made king (2 Samuel 2:1-4).

10. When the Spirit told him to join himself to the chariot of the Ethiopian eunuch, he immediately ran up to it (Acts 8:26-40).

11. He went and dwelt by the brook Cherith during the famine, as the Lord commanded (1 Kings 17:1-5).

12. He purposed in his heart not to defile himself in Babylon by partaking of the king's food (Daniel 1:1-8).

13. He was allowed to enter the promised land because he "wholly followed the Lord" (Numbers 32:11, 12).

14. God commended him as a faithful servant, more meek than any man on the face of the earth at that time (Numbers 12:3-8).

```
 1.          _ E  T  _  _
 2.             _ O  _  H
 3.       _ A  T  _  _  _
 4.       _  _ A  _  _  H
 5.       _  _ U  L
 6.          _ O  _  _  U  _
 7.          _ B  R  _  _
 8.       _  _  _ E  _  I  _  _
 9.    _ A  _  _ D
10.       _  _ I  L  _  _
11.          E  _  _ J  _  _
12.       D  _ N  _  _  _
13.          C  _  _  _ B
14.       _ O  _ E  _
```

EARLY ISRAEL

For they all seek their own interests, not those of Jesus Christ.
—Philippians 2:21 (ESV)

Back when I was in my midtwenties, I had just completed four years in the military and started looking for a job. With a math degree, I thought I knew what was best and before long was employed in an office position. It seemed right, but due to some unforeseen circumstances, I wound up working there only a couple of weeks. Discouraged, I began to earnestly pray for guidance, and the Lord eventually led me to a tutoring position in the field of education. Later, I went back to school to earn a graduate degree and start my teaching career.

The book of Judges describes dark times during the early years of the nation of Israel. Time and time again, the people suffered oppression at the hands of surrounding nations. Each time they cried to the Lord for help, He raised up a judge through which deliverance came. But it was not long before the nation again drifted away from God, repeating the same cycle. The main reason for this is outlined in the last verse of the book. Here we read, "In those days there was no king in Israel; everyone did what was right in his own eyes" (Judges 21:25 NKJV).

How often, as in my employment situation years ago, we think we know what is right and then wonder why things do not work out the way we believe they should. We need to search after God wholeheartedly and surrender to Him (Luke 9:23). So much heartache will be avoided, and so much blessing will result.

JUDGE FOR YOURSELF

In ancient Israel, the people continually drifted away from God in disobedience. Thus they ran into trouble, usually in the form of oppression by foreign nations. Yet the Lord was merciful. When the people cried out to Him, He raised up judges to deliver them. When we are troubled, the Lord can deliver us as well. Let us, however, learn from the past. Often we can save ourselves much unnecessary difficulty if we obey God in the first place.

Fill in this puzzle. All answers are names of judges of ancient Israel. Numbers 13 and 15 are found in 1 Samuel. The others are all found in the book of Judges.

Across:
1. put a fleece before God (6:36-40)
4. nephew of Caleb (3:9-11)
10. judged with Deborah (4:6-9)
11. a prophetess (4:4)
12. slew six hundred Philistines with an ox goad (3:31)
13. anointed Saul as first king (9:17; 10:1)
15. sons in gross sin (2:22-25)
16. loved Delilah (16:3, 4)

Down:
2. a Zebulonite (12:11, 12)
3. made a vow unto the Lord (11:30, 31)
5. from Issachar (10:1, 2)

6. killed Eglon king of Moab (3:15-21)
7. a Gileadite (10:3-5)
8. had thirty sons and thirty daughters (12:8-10)
9. murdered seventy people in one place (9:4, 5)
14. followed Elon as judge (12:12, 13)

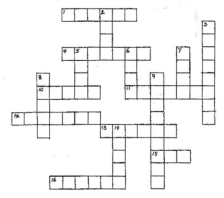

DAVID

I have a part-time job grading high school math exams from a correspondence school. I receive exams from all across the country and even overseas. Most exams arrive in good condition, but on occasion, I have to grade papers that we call "soiled." That is, they may have suffered water damage, contain coffee stains, or been dirtied up in some other way. Sometimes I wonder what I am looking at and hesitate to touch them without wearing plastic gloves. When this occurs, students are notified, and occasionally they have to resend their work.

Though not perfect, King David was said to be a man after God's own heart (Acts 13:22). When he committed sin, he was quick to repent and ask the Lord's forgiveness. Read Psalm 51. In verse 9, David asked God to hide His face from his sin and to blot out all of his iniquities. God answered his contrite prayer. There were consequences for his actions (see 2 Samuel 12:1–14), but David was forgiven.

Just like soiled papers ruin otherwise good exams, sins mar God's work on our behalf. Let us be like David. If we confess our sins, the Lord promises to cleanse and forgive us (1 John 1:9). Our lives, "soiled by sin" (see Isaiah 1:18), are then made pure and whole.

HEART EXAM

"For the word of God . . . is a discerner of the thoughts and intents of the heart" (Hebrew 4:12). "Keep thy heart with all diligence; for out of it are the issues of life" (Proverbs 4:23). "For there is nothing covered, that shall not be revealed; neither hid, that shall not be known" (Luke 12:2). The Lord knows your heart. Examine it today. Is it pure in His sight?

In the puzzle below you will find fifteen words describing thoughts or attitudes you must guard yourself against. Circle them as you discover them, either backwards, forwards, across, down, or diagonal. After you are finished, the remaining letters will spell out a simple way to keep your heart pure before God (Philippians 4:8). Read these Scriptures if you need help: Philippians 2:14; James 3:16; 1 John 4:18; Romans 1:29; Revelation 2:9; Proverbs 15:27; 1 Timothy 4:2; 1 John 2:16; 1 Samuel 15:23; John 15:18; Hebrews 12:15

```
M  U  R  M  U  R  I  N  G  S
T  H  E  N  V  Y  I  N  S  N
R  A  E  F  G  S  T  E  I  O
L  K  O  N  R  I  N  D  D  I
M  U  R  D  E  R  S  I  O  L
H  G  S  C  E  C  T  R  L  L
O  A  E  T  D  O  R  P  A  E
O  D  T  D  T  P  I  H  T  B
I  I  N  E  G  Y  F  S  R  E
B  L  A  S  P  H  E  M  Y  R
```

Letters spell out: _____

27

KINGDOMS OF ISRAEL AND JUDAH

Many believers, even though saved, continue to struggle with sin. Often we vow to stop our sinful behaviors only to repeat the same offenses over and over again. Could this perpetual defeat be because we so often approach the sin problem in the wrong way?

King Rehoboam was the son of King Solomon. A very interesting verse concerning him states the following: "And he did evil because he did not prepare his heart to seek the Lord" (2 Chronicles 12:14 NKJV). His problem was not because of what he did but rather because of what he did not do. Failure to seek God results in wrong behavior. Galatians 5:16 says that if we walk in the Spirit, *then* we will not fulfill the desires of the flesh. Instead of trying to defeat sin through our own efforts, in a vain attempt to please God, let us concentrate on seeking Him. Victory comes through Jesus alone (1 Corinthians 15:57). If we surrender daily to the Lord, the sin problem will be dealt with properly.

Many years later, another king named Hezekiah reigned over Judah. Unlike King Rehoboam, according to 2 Chronicles 31:21, Hezekiah sought God with all of his heart, and he prospered. Let us follow his example. Victory and God's favor will result.

A ROYAL PROBLEM

Nations of the earth often rise and fall as a direct result of their leadership. A godly ruler will encourage God's favor upon his entire nation. Conversely, an evil dictator may drive his nation to ruin. Examples of this are found not only in the Bible but also in modern times as well. We must pray for our leaders.

Complete the following crossword puzzle regarding Old Testament monarchs. All "across" answers refer to kings of ancient Israel, all "down" answers refer to kings of ancient Judah.

Across:
2. murdered by Baasha (1 Kings 15:25-27)
5. first king of separated Israel (1 Kings 12:20)
8. reigned only one month (2 Kings 15:13)
10. evil husband of Jezebel (1 Kings 16:29-31)
11. murderer, reigned only seven days (1 Kings 16:15, 16)
13. last king before exile to Assyria (2 Kings 17:1-6)
14. anointed king by the command of Elisha (2 Kings 9:1-3)
15. son of Ahab, evil two-year reign (1 Kings 22:51-53)

Down:
1. Solomon's son (1 Kings 14:21)
3. good forty-one year reign (1 Kings 15:10, 11)
4. entered into agreement with Ahab (2 Chronicles 18:1-3)
6. prayed against Sennacherib king of Assyria (2 Kings 19:14-19)
7. son of Hezekiah, evil reign (2 Kings 21:1-3)
9. wrongly burned incense in the temple, became a leper (2 Chronicles 26:18-21)
12. father of Hezekiah, evil reign (2 Kings 16:1-4, 20)
14. escaped being killed by Athaliah (2 Kings 11:2)

ISRAEL IN EXILE

If you read the book of Esther, you will notice something very surprising. This is the only book of the Bible in which God is not specifically mentioned. Yes, there was effective fasting, and the Jews (in exile from their land) experienced extraordinary deliverance from what appeared to be certain annihilation. But nowhere is there any direct reference to God throughout the entire text. You could say that the Lord was working behind the scenes.

How often we complain when we pray about certain things and appear not to receive answers. Assuming known sin is confessed and we are sincere in seeking God, it can be frustrating when we do not receive what we wish for. Our tendency is to assume that God did not hear or does not care. We then become discouraged. Appropriately, one translation of *Esther* is "something hidden." God is always active on our behalf, whether we see it or not. What may be currently hidden will be brought to light in due course. Read Jeremiah 33:3. The God who works behind the scenes is able to do great and mighty things.

WAIT ON THE LORD

One of the most difficult things for children of God to learn is patience. It has been said that more Christians give up on the Lord through impatience than through anything else. Learn to wait on God for His perfect timing. "But let patience have her perfect work, that ye may be perfect and entire, wanting nothing" (James 1:4).

You cannot "rush through" this puzzle! Patiently take the time to look up each verse in order to match the correct Scripture to its promise. Draw lines to match them correctly.

Scripture	Promise to You
1. Psalm 25:3	A. receive power through the Holy Spirit
2. Psalm 27:14	B. save you
3. Psalm 33:20	C. not be ashamed
4. Psalm 37:34	D. shall not be moved
5. Psalm 62:5, 6	E. renew your strength
6. Proverbs 20:22	F. strengthen your heart
7. Isaiah 40:31	G. exalt you to inherit the land
8. Isaiah 64:4	H. protect you
9. Acts 1:4-8	I. unusual future blessing
10. 1 Thessalonians 1:10	J. deliver you from the wrath to come

DANIEL

When I grade math papers, I always check to make sure that students show proper work toward their solutions. If answers, the way I put it, "magically appear," then points are lost. No matter who the student is or how well liked he or she may be, I will not put up with sloppy or missing work. Grades will suffer. On this point I remain consistent.

When it came to obedience to God, the Old Testament prophet Daniel was remarkably consistent. After being deported to Babylon, the young man refused to eat meat sacrificed to idols. As a result, along with his other faithful companions, he was granted favor (Daniel 1:8–16). Later in life, he was put to a greater test. Despite a contrived law conceived by jealous people in order to trap him, Daniel continued to pray to God three times a day—despite the potential consequences. He was caught and thrown into a loins' den but was miraculously protected (see Daniel chapter 6).

We may not be tested to the extremes Daniel experienced, but, like him, let us strive to remain faithful and consistent in our obedience to the Lord. He will honor that and bless us as a result.

YOUNG AND
OLD ALIKE

All too often people tend to limit God. Young people who are inexperienced are afraid to step out in faith; some elderly people declining in strength feel they've outlived their usefulness. But regardless of age, God can use you as you yield to Him. Be faithful to do what He tells you and fruitfulness will result.

Below are listed the names of fifteen different people along with dramatic events which greatly influenced their lives. By letter, match the correct age of each.

Person	Event	Age
1. ____ Jesus (Luke 3:21-23)	baptized by the Holy Spirit	A. 12
2. ____ Joash (2 Chronicles 24:1)	became king over Judah	B. 25
3. ____ Abraham (Genesis 21:5)	Isaac born	C. 600
4. ____ Joseph (Genesis 37:2-28)	sold as a slave to the Egyptians	D. 85
5. ____ Noah (Genesis 7:6)	beginning of the flood	E. over 40
6. ____ David (2 Samuel 5:4)	began reign as king	F. 7
7. ____ Caleb (Joshua 14:6-14)	inherited the land	G. 365
8. ____ Jeremiah (Jeremiah 1:1-5)	ordained a prophet to the nations	H. before his birth
9. ____ Moses (Exodus 7:1-7)	appeared before Pharaoh in the power of God	I. 60

10. ____ Enoch   taken after walking   J. about 30
    (Genesis 5:23,   with God
    24)

11. ____ Jairus'   raised from the   K. 100
    daughter   dead
    (Luke 8:41, 42,
    49-56)

12. ____ lame man   healed   L. 17
    by the temple
    (Acts 3:1-10;
    4:22)

13. ____ Hezekiah   became king   M. over 91
    (2 Kings 18:1, 2)   over Judah

14. ____ Isaac   birth of Esau   N. 30
    (Genesis   and Jacob
    25:21-26)

15. ____ Anna   prophesied over   O. 80
    (Luke 2:34-38)   the Christ child

JOB

Most of us are familiar with the story of Job. Throughout all of his suffering, he did not understand why such awful things were happening to him. Of course, we know why—because in Job chapters 1 and 2 we are told what took place between the Lord and Satan. God knew what He was doing, and because Job maintained his integrity, his fortunes were restored. He ended up with twice as much as he had before.

During the time of the prophet Elisha, we are given another glimpse of the heavenly realm (see 2 Kings 6:8–18). A foreign king sent troops to surround and capture Elisha. His servant was fearful, so Elisha asked the Lord to open his eyes. He saw that the mountain was full of horses, with chariots of fire all around them to protect them.

It is easy for us to react the way Job and Elisha's servant did. This is because we are focused only on what we see. However, according to 2 Corinthians 4:18, things that are seen are only temporary, but things that are unseen are eternal. Trust God no matter what. Like Job, if we do not understand what is happening in our lives but remain faithful, eternal blessing will be the result in the end.

OUR UNSEEN WORLD

"The things which are seen are temporal but the things which are not seen are eternal" (2 Corinthians 4:18). It is all too common for us to view our surroundings with sense knowledge only. However, the Lord desires that we broaden our vision to include the ever important world we do not see. Our eyes may not behold it, but it is very real indeed.

Below are mentioned a number of things the Bible says exist even though we don't see them. You must crack the code in order to *see* them here.

Example: Y M J   Q T W I   N X   F Y   R D   W N L M Y   M F S I

THE LORD IS AT MY RIGHT HAND (Psalm 16:8)

1. Y M J   I J A N Q   F X   F   W T F W N S L   Q N T S,
    B F Q P X   F G T Z Y,   X J J P N S L   B M T R   M J
    R F D   I J A T Z W

2. Y M J   Q T W I   K N Q Q X   M J F A J S   F S I   J F W Y M

3. Y M J   X U N W N Y   T K   L T I   I B J Q Q X   N S   D T Z

4. B M J W J   Y B T   T W   Y M W J J   F W J   L F Y M J W J I
    Y T L J Y M J W   N S   O J X Z X'   S F R J,   M J   N X
    N S Y M J N W   R N I X Y

5. B J   B W J X Y Q J   F L F N S X Y   X U N W N Y Z F Q
    W Z Q J W X   T K   I F W P S J X X   N S   M N L M
    U Q F H J X

6. FSLJQX RNSNXYJW KTW YMJR BMT
   FWJ MJNWX TK XFQAFYNTS

7. BJ FWJ XZWWTZSIJI GD F LWJFY
   HQTZI TK BNYSJXXJX

8. NS MJQQ YMJ BTWR SJAJW INJX
   FSI YMJ KNWJ NX SJAJW VZJSHMJI

9. OJXZX NX XJY ITBS FY YMJ WNLMY
   MSFI TK YMJ YMWTSJ TK LTI

10. YMJ QTWI XNYX ZUTS HNWHQJ TK
    YMJ JFWYM

PSALMS AND PROVERBS

Oh, give thanks to the Lord, for He is good! For His mercy endures
forever. Let the redeemed of the Lord say so.
—Psalm 107:1–2 (NKJV)

Sabina Wurmbrand, wife of Richard Wurmbrand (founder of the Voice
of the Martyrs), was imprisoned for three years in Communist Romania.
Her story is told in the book *Wurmbrand: Tortured for Christ—The
Complete Story*. She not only had to endure beatings and mockery by the
Communists but also curses by unbelieving cellmates, which almost drove
her to despair. Her small Christian group, having no Bible, asked the Lord
how they could possibly deal with this. One of them, a young girl, shared
a scripture passage she had memorized. It was from Psalm 107. The results
were remarkable. No matter what their circumstances were, the Christian
ladies always greeted one another with these words: "Give thanks to the
Lord, for He is good, and His mercy endures forever." They received the
faith, courage, and strength they needed to make it through each day.

Read Psalm 136. What do each of the twenty-six verses of this psalm have
in common? All end with the same declaration (NKJV): "For His mercy
endures forever." Is the Lord trying to tell us something? No matter what
you are going through, always remind yourself that God's grace and mercy
will sustain you. It will last forever.

STEPPING THROUGH PSALMS

Write in the correct psalm number for each statement below. Numbers to choose from will be found at the end of the puzzle. If done correctly, the letters accompanying each of the numbers will, in order, spell out what the book of Psalms is all about!

1. _____ The Lord is my shepherd.
2. _____ Let every thing that hath breath praise the Lord.
3. _____ The longest chapter of the entire Bible.
4. _____ Trust ... delight ... in the Lord; and he shall give thee the desires of thine heart.
5. _____ A psalm written by Moses.
6. _____ The Lord of Hosts, he is the King of glory.
7. _____ Search me, O God, and know my heart ... and lead me in the way everlasting.
8. _____ Pray for the peace of Jerusalem.
9. _____ But his delight is in the law of the Lord; and in his law doth he meditate day and night.
10. _____ The shortest chapter in the entire Bible.
11. _____ Neither wilt thou suffer thine Holy One to see corruption.
12. _____ The angel of the Lord encampeth round about them that fear him, and delivereth them.
13. _____ Create in me a clean heart, O God; and renew a right spirit within me.
14. _____ Enter into his gates with thanksgiving, and into his courts with praise.

Psalms to choose from:

1—R	37—O	119—O
16—I	51—E	122—P
23—A	90—K	139—F
24—O	100—S	150—B
34—S	117—A	

A WALK THROUGH PROVERBS

Everyone desires wisdom and common sense. In order to achieve them, read a few proverbs every day. You will know what to do and how to act in every circumstance if you meditate on this remarkable book.

Answer each of the following questions, all based on the book of Proverbs.

1. Who wrote most of the proverbs? (1:1)

2. Why were the proverbs written? (1:2–6)

3. How are those who refuse the Lord's wisdom and counsel punished? (1:29–31)

4. What happens when we honor the Lord with the first fruits of our wealth? (3:9–10)

5. What is the last of the seven things the Lord says He hates? (6:16–19)

6. What is the difference between reproving a scorner (scoffer) and reproving a wise man? (9:8)

7. What do the proverbs have to say regarding godly counsel? (11:14, 24:6)

8. A certain way may seem right to a person, but what is the outcome? (14:12)

9. Grievous words stir up anger. What turns anger away? (15:1)

10. What is the outcome of gossip? (17:9)

11. Why is it very important for us to watch what we say? (18:21)

12. Political leaders exert great influence. What does the Lord have to say about them? (21:1)

13. Scripture exhorts us to train up children in the way they should go. What is God's promise if we do so? (22:6)

14. How important are our innermost thoughts? (23:7)

15. What is the outcome of people without a vision? (29:18)

16. What is the outcome for a virtuous, godly woman? (31:28–30)

OLD TESTAMENT PROPHETS

One day, I arranged for a technician to come to my home to repair my water heater. While he was working on it, I was writing with a red pen. He asked what I was doing. I told him I taught math and was grading calculus exams. He then said, "Oh my, that is way out of my league." I pointed out that the same applied to me. He could not understand calculus, but I could not fix my water heater.

All of us possess unique God-given talents and abilities. Jeremiah, a famous Old Testament prophet, was told by the Lord that He knew him even before he was formed in the womb and that before he was born, he was ordained to be a prophet to the nations (Jeremiah 1:5).

God had a great plan for Jeremiah, and He has a great plan for you. The Bible says, "Eye has not seen, nor ear heard, nor have entered into the heart of man the things which God has prepared for those who love Him" (1 Corinthians 2:9 NKJV). Jeremiah 29:11 declares that God plans for you a good future and a hope.

Perhaps you never thought about such a plan but wish to know it. Pray about it. Think of what you are good at and what you like doing. Ask other believers you know for godly input. The Lord may not reveal everything at once, but He promises to guide you step by step (Proverbs 16:9). Finding God's purpose and fulfilling it brings great satisfaction. You and others are blessed, and He is glorified.

PROPHECY FULFILLED

It is said that the odds of Jesus having fulfilled just ten Old Testament prophecies "by chance" are so astronomically high as to be virtually impossible. Yet he fulfilled many more than that! And He did so in great detail. The lesson is clear: Christ is who He says He is, and the Bible is true. It takes incredible "faith" to believe otherwise!

By letter, match up each passage of prophecy and fulfillment listed below with the correct statement about Jesus.

Prophecy

A. Zechariah 9:9
B. Isaiah 50:6
C. Psalm 2:7
D. Psalm 22:17, 18
E. Zechariah 12:10
F. Micah 5:2
G. Isaiah 9:7
H. Psalm 41:9
I. Psalm 35:11
J. Isaiah 7:14
K. Psalm 69:21
L. Psalm 16:10
M. Zechariah 11:12
N. Isaiah 53:9
O. Genesis 49:10
P. Psalm 34:20
Q. Isaiah 53:3

Fulfillment

A. John 1:11
B. Luke 2:4-7
C. Luke 3:33
D. Mark 16:6, 7
E. Matthew 3:17
F. Matthew 26:67
G. Luke 22:47, 48
H. John 19:33, 36
I. Matthew 27:34
J. Luke 1:32, 33
K. Mark 14:57, 58
L. Luke 1:26-31
M. Matthew 27:57-60
N. Mark 11:7-11
O. John 19:34
P. Matthew 27:35, 36
Q. Matthew 26:15

Prophecy		Fulfillment
_____	1. from the tribe of Judah	_____
_____	2. heir to the throne of David	_____
_____	3. born in Bethlehem	_____
_____	4. born of a virgin	_____
_____	5. declared the Son of God	_____
_____	6. rejected by His people	_____
_____	7. triumphal entry into Jerusalem	_____
_____	8. betrayed	_____
_____	9. sold for thirty pieces of silver	_____
_____	10. accused by false witnesses	_____
_____	11. spat upon and smitten	_____
_____	12. side pierced	_____
_____	13. given vinegar to drink	_____
_____	14. soldiers gambled for His coat	_____
_____	15. no broken bones	_____
_____	16. buried in a rich man's grave	_____
_____	17. resurrected	_____

OLD TESTAMENT MIRACLES

Oh no! I thought. I had misplaced the form I needed in order to claim a state refund, and the deadline to file it was fast approaching (this was before the internet, so I could not simply look it up and print another one). I looked all over for the required form but could not find it. Eventually, I gave up the search. Assuming the money was lost, I prayed that if by some miracle I located it and was able to send it off in time, I'd give the money away. The day before the Friday deadline filing date, I stumbled upon the form in a place I didn't figure it would be! So I quickly filled it out and sent it off in the mail late Thursday afternoon. The following Tuesday (in only five days, counting a weekend), from the state government, a check for the entire amount was in my mailbox! How quickly this happened was a miracle in itself. So, as I promised the Lord, I gave the money away to a needy charitable organization. About a week later at work, I received an unexpected bonus exactly four times the original amount!

This may not be quite as miraculous as provision for a widow during the time of the prophet Elijah (you can read about it in 1 Kings 17:8–16), but the principle is the same. If we give away, especially sacrificially, God will give back (Luke 6:38), often in ways we do not expect. He was and still is a miracle-working God!

MIRACLES OF OLD

The many miracles of God as described in the Old Testament make for fascinating reading. But can the Old Testament be relied upon for accuracy? "Thy word is true from the beginning ..." (Psalm 119:160). Could such miracles happen today? "For I am the Lord, I change not..." (Malachi 3:6).

As you read the following passages you will be reminded of no less than twenty specific Old Testament miracles of God. Can you recall them all? List as many as you can find in the blanks provided at the conclusion of the puzzle.

A. It happened because the boys departed the premises carelessly, not having completely put out the campfire. One hot cinder was blown onto a nearby bush and set it on fire. Before long the entire forest was ablaze. Firefighters rushed to the scene but there was little they could do. When great burning trees collapsed to the ground it was as if fire fell from the sky. Three firemen appeared trapped in a blazing inferno, but somehow managed to escape. From a distance the entire mountain appeared to quake as thick dark smoke ascended into the sky. It was an awesome sight.

B. It was young Teddy's first visit to the zoo, and he

was exited. Never before had he seen so many different types of animals.

"How I wish I could talk to them, and they to me" he remarked as he passed by donkeys, zebras, and giraffes. "I bet they'd have a lot to say."

"It would be difficult to speak to all of them" replied his sister. "They all speak different languages, you know."

Not wishing to miss a single animal, Teddy was disappointed as he looked into what appeared to be an empty cage. Only at the last moment did he notice the snake, which blended in so well with the background it appeared at first as a long, narrow stick. Teddy got into trouble when he ventured too close to the lion's cage, and he was yanked back quickly amidst the shrieks of his parents as well as onlookers. Other than that, he thoroughly enjoyed himself and was quite sad when it came time to return home.

C. At first only one small cloud, appearing as a man's hand, arose out of the sea to the west. However, it loomed larger and larger as it moved eastward until finally the entire sky was darkened. Rain began to fall and before long a ferocious storm battered the coast. The jetty parted the waters on both sides but could not halt the onslaught of the huge waves, which smashed into rocks, sending spray high into the air. All along the coast there was extensive flooding, as many homes had to be evacuated. Pounding surf and wind even caused the walls of beach homes to collapse. Great fish were washed ashore and debris was strewn about everywhere. It was one of the worst storms on record.

D. It was a beautiful spring morning. The stark, bare trees had begun to bud and blossom. Dew, which drenched the ground, began to evaporate beneath the warm rays of the sun. The melodious sound of singing birds filled the air. As long shadows slowly receded along the sundial in the back yard, one almost wished time would stand still. It was so peaceful.

Miracles:

1. _____
2. _____
3. _____
4. _____
5. _____
6. _____
7. _____
8. _____
9. _____
10. _____
11. _____
12. _____
13. _____

14. _____

15. _____

16. _____

17. _____

18. _____

19. _____

20. _____

THE GOSPELS

As one reads through the Gospels (the first four books of the New Testament), it is obvious from the text that Jesus is human but also claims to be divine. Believers accept this by faith. But how, some ask, do we know that the Gospels are actually true? Is Jesus really who He claims to be? Let us briefly explore this through an unlikely source: mathematics.

We know that certain Roman numerals also represent numbers: V = 5, X = 10, and so on. The same is true for all letters of the Greek and Hebrew alphabets. In Luke 2:21, if you add up the numerical equivalents of the Greek letters that spell "Jesus," your total is 888. In Isaiah 52:10 of the Old Testament, the phrase "salvation of our God" (in Hebrew) adds up to the same number: 888! Incidentally, the number 8 in biblical terms represents the number of new beginnings. There are seven days in a week, so the eighth day begins a new week. The musical scale consists of seven notes; the next (eighth) note begins a new scale. Eight is also said to be the resurrection number. How appropriate!

The Greek numerical equivalent of "Lord Jesus Christ" is 3,168. It is interesting to note the following:

(1) On earth, we dwell within the lithosphere (earth's crust) and atmosphere (air above), which totals approximately 60 miles, and 60 mi x 5,280 ft/mi is 316,800 feet. "For in Him we live, and move, and have our being" (Acts 17:28).

(2) The average distance from the earth to the sun is 93,000,000 miles. Converting this to inches and then dividing by the speed of light, 186,000 miles per second, gives an answer of 3.168×10 to the 7th power. If the sun were any closer to or farther away from the earth than it actually is, life on our planet would not exist.

(3) The diameter of the earth is 7,920 miles. A square enclosing the earth would have a perimeter of 7920 x 4 = 31,680 miles.

(4) The latitude of Bethlehem is 31.68 degrees north.

There are many other mathematical patterns within scripture, so many that it is virtually impossible for all of them to have happened by chance. It appears that our Creator has left His mathematical signature. How marvelous He is!

GLIMPSING THE GOSPELS

Some people feel that once they've read something a first time, they know it all, and there is no need for review. This is not true, especially regarding the Bible. No matter how many times you've read through scripture, if you are open to it, God is able to reveal something new to you that you never noticed before. Any time you read a passage of scripture, it is only a glimpse at best.

How well do you really know the Gospels? See how many of the following questions you can answer, all of which come from the first four books of the New Testament.

1. What is the name of the angel who appeared to Mary, explaining to her that she would be the mother of Jesus?

2. What man blessed God upon seeing the child Jesus in the temple in Jerusalem? The Lord revealed to him that, before he died, he would see the Messiah.

3. When Herod determined to have the child Jesus killed, to what nation did Joseph and Mary take Him to safety?

4. Only one of Jesus's miracles (apart from His resurrection) is mentioned in all four of the Gospels. Do you know which one?

5. One of Jesus's most famous miracles occurred when He walked on the sea and when Peter did likewise. What other incredible miracle happened immediately after that?

6. We all know who Judas was (the traitor). Can you name his father?

7. Many people, grateful to be healed by Jesus, desired to follow along with Him. Yet in one famous case, Jesus gave a certain man the chance to follow Him, but he refused to do so. Who was this?

8. As Jesus was being arrested, a certain young man followed Him. When people tried to seize him, he ran off. What was so unusual about this?

9. A person named Cleopas is not mentioned until after Jesus rose from the dead. Who was he?

10. As soon as we pray for salvation through belief in Christ, the Holy Spirit comes to reside in us (see John 3:5 as well as Romans 8:9–10). Before He ascended to the Father, how did Jesus impart the Spirit to His disciples?

ACTS

I remember an early evening long ago when I entered a spiritual discussion with my cousin who was not yet a believer. As we talked about the Lord, I said, "Don't wait to make a decision to receive Jesus as your Savior. Nobody knows the future. At any moment, without warning, your life could be snuffed out," snapping my fingers. At that precise instant, a timed lamp in the room turned off, and the room became dark. Both of us were shocked! My cousin then said, "This is more or less what I was looking for." He believed at that moment.

If you read the book of Acts, you will notice that it seems to be incomplete. That is, there is no proper ending. Many believe this is because the story is not yet finished. What started with the apostles two thousand years ago still continues. That is, people are getting saved, and lives are being continually transformed to this very day. Especially in what we call the developing world, signs and wonders, including miraculous healings, are reportedly taking place. Whether through physical healing or a light shut off at the snap of a finger, God knows what people need in order to draw them to Him.

The book of Acts, however, someday will be completed when the Lord's promised return takes place. According to 2 Corinthians 6:2, now is the day of salvation. If you have not yet trusted Jesus to save you, there is no time better than the present.

THIS IS YOUR MISSION

Perhaps the greatest missionary of all time was the apostle Paul. He traveled extensively to share the gospel at a time when modern methods of transportation were unavailable, and he suffered numerous hardships. Yet many people turned to Christ as a result of his preaching. Through the inspiration of the Holy Spirit, he wrote much of our New Testament. Read for yourself, about the journeys of Paul, and above all strive to learn from his example.

Your "mission" is: Fill in the names of each of the places described below. All are connected with one or more of Paul's missionary journeys. All references are from the book of Acts.

Paul:

1. addressed the Ephesian elders here (20:17, 18).
2. began his first journey form here (13:1-3).
3. was received by Jason here (17: 1-7).
4. was forbidden to preach here (16:3-6).
5. witnessed here to a believing jailer (16:12-34).
6. fled from here to Lystra and Derbe (14:1-6).
7. met and lived with Aquila and Priscilla here (18:1-3).
8. abode at Philip's home here (21:8).
9. first met Timothy here (16:1).
10. was stoned here (14:8-19).
11. desired to be here at Pentecost (20:16).
12. was guided here by a vision (16:8-10).
13. was imitated by the seven sons of Sceva here (19:13-17).

14. saw John Mark depart from him here (13:13).
15. preached on Mars' hill here (17:22).
16. fled here from Thessalonica (17:10, 11).
17. silenced Elymas the sorcerer on this isle (13:4-12).

```
 1.                      M  __ __ __ __ __ __ __
 2,              __ __ __ I  __ __ __
 3.           __ __ __ __ S  __ __ __ __ __ __ __
 4.              __ __ __ S  __ __ __
 5.              __ __ __ I  __ __ __ __ __
 6.           __    __ __ O  __ __ __ __ __
 7. __ __ __     __ __ N  __ __
 8. __ __ __        __ __ A  __    __      __      __
 9.              __ __ R  __ __ __
10.              __ Y
```

```
11.                      J  __ __ __ __ __ __ __ __
12.              __ __ __ O  __ __
13. __ __ __ __ __ __ U  __
14.              __ __ R  __ __ __
15.           __ __ __ __ N  __
16.              __ __ E  __ __ __ __
17.              __ Y  __ __ __ __
```

PAUL

I teach college math, and for each class, I am required to give a final exam at the end of the semester. This is a way of assessing how well my students know what they have learned and how prepared they are to continue their education. Some students spend quality time to prepare well for this exam. Other students put forth little effort. As they say, some study hard, while others hardly study. When I give out final grades, the former are rewarded for their efforts, and the latter pay the price through low grades or even course failure.

Did you know that all of us have to face a final exam some day? "And as it is appointed unto men once to die, but after this the judgment" (Hebrews 9:27). The apostle Paul was well aware of this. His ultimate goal was to serve and please God above all else. Carefully read about this in Philippians chapter 3. He also spoke about what we call the judgment seat of Christ (2 Corinthians 5:10). All believers will have to stand before Jesus and give account for their lives. It is not a matter of salvation (that is assured; see John 5:24). It has to do with reward. Those who are spiritually prepared will be greatly rewarded. The spiritually lazy will suffer loss (1 Corinthians 3:12–15).

College students who fail a class have a chance to retake it, but only one life is lived, followed by one final exam. What type of foundation are you building upon? There is an old saying: only that which is done for Christ will last. How true that is.

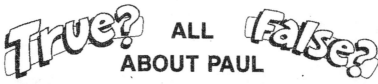# True? ALL False? ABOUT PAUL

Paul was perhaps the greatest apostle of the early church. Few could sincerely claim as he did, "Those things, which ye have both learned, and received, and heard, and seen in me, do" (Philippians 4:9). Read his epistles and take heed to Paul's teachings. God will bless you for it.

How much do you know about the apostle Paul? Answer each of the following true or false.

1. ____ Paul's previous name was Saul (Acts 13:9).

2. ____ Paul was converted through a visitation of the Lord while on his way to Jerusalem (Acts 9:1-6).

3. ____ Paul was a Roman citizen (Acts 22:25, 26).

4. ____ Paul was considered a member of the Pharisees (Acts 23:6).

5. ____ When Peter withdrew from the Gentiles in favor of Jewish believers, Paul commended him first (Galatians 1:1; 2:11-14).

6. ____ Paul's testimony to the masses in Jerusalem was well received (Acts 22:1-24).

7. ____ Paul never had moments of weakness or fear (1 Corinthians 1:1, 2; 2:3)

8. ____ Paul wrote the epistle to the Colossians (Colossians 1:1, 2).

9. ____ Paul disputed with Barnabas as to whether to take Timothy along on his second missionary journey (Acts 15:36-40).

10. ____ Paul once preached in Athens (Acts 17:16-34).

11. ____ Paul showed great love for his unsaved coun-
trymen (Romans 1:1; 9:1-5).

12. ____ In order to meet his needs, Paul often worked
as a fisherman (Acts 18:1-3).

13. ____ During a shipwreck, it was Paul who encouraged the others, even though he was a pris-
oner (Acts 27:29-44).

14. ____ Paul actually sang praises to God while un-
justly bound in a prison (Acts 16:14-25).

15. ____ Paul baptized many new converts (1 Corinthians 1:13-17).

16. ____ Paul often reasoned with the Jews concerning
Jesus according to the Scriptures (Acts 17:1,
2).

17. ____ Paul was once caught up into Heaven and
then returned (2 Corinthians 1:1; 12:2-7).

18. ____ Paul was stoned to death at Lystra (Acts 14:8-
20).

19. ____ Paul believed in salvation by grace (salvation
being an unearned gift from God) (Ephesians
1:1; 2:8, 9).

20. ____ Paul had a great burden for those saved
through his ministry (2 Corinthians 1:1; 11:28,
29).

THE EPISTLES

It was the Tuesday before Thanksgiving. I left my office at the university, entered the parking lot, and got into my car to begin my commute home. However, there was a problem. My car would not start. I thought it might be the battery, but that turned out not to be the case. I had to have the car towed to a repair facility. After my initial frustration, however, I sensed something unusual. Instead of anxiety, I was at peace. The Lord assured me that everything would all work out. And that is exactly what happened. The math department secretary graciously drove me home. On Thanksgiving Day, I thought I could not attend a holiday meal with church friends, but one of them went out of his way to pick me up and drive me home afterward. My next-door neighbor took me to the repair shop on Friday to pick up my car. I had the money in the bank to pay the bill. Throughout it all, God provided and granted me His peace.

If you observe carefully, what common thread do you notice within the first four verses of the first chapter of every one of Paul's epistles, as well as letters from Peter, John (in 2 John), and Jude? Grace and peace are proclaimed upon the letter's recipients. God does not want us to worry or be fearful. He is always in control. Peace is a part of the fruit of God's Spirit, as stated by Paul in Galatians 5:22. May God's peace, which surpasses understanding (Philippians 4:7), be yours in abundance as you thank and praise Him.

EXHORTATION
EXERCISE

In both Romans and Thessalonians, the apostle Paul exhorts us to walk in a manner worthy of the calling of the Lord. Choose one of Paul's admonitions and begin today to apply it to your life. God always rewards those who honor His Word and seek to obey it.

Arrange the following words from 1 Thessalonians 5 in correct order to reveal Paul's admonitions to the Thessalonians.

1. evermore rejoice _____ (16)

2. not prophesyings despise _____ (20)

3. pray ceasing without _____ (17)

4. the quench Spirit not _____ (19)

5. all from of appearance abstain evil _____

   _____ (22)

6. fast prove things which hold good is that all _____

   _____ (21)

7. give you is in will this Jesus God Christ every concerning of thanks thing for the in _____

   _____ (18)

NEW TESTAMENT MIRACLES

As we know, the Gospels record that Jesus performed many miracles during His time on earth. Miracles of healing, deliverance, provision—He did so much that the apostle John said that the world could not contain all the books that could be written about them (John 21:25). However, there was one place where Jesus did very little—in His own hometown of Nazareth. Why was this so? It was because of their unbelief (see Mark 6:1–6). The same problem plagued the children of Israel after their miraculous deliverance from the hands of the Egyptians many years before. Despite all that God had done on their behalf, the people complained and refused to believe in Him. They suffered greatly as a result (read Psalm 78, also Hebrews 3:16–19).

Nothing is impossible with God (Luke 1:37). He always knows what is best and has good things planned for each of us. Let us learn from scripture and not limit Him by unbelief.

IT'S A MIRACLE

"The same works that I do, bear witness of me, that the Father hath sent me" (John 5:36). One way in which Jesus Christ revealed His divinity was through the mighty miracles which He performed. When these miracles occurred, man was blessed and God was glorified.

Use the clues provided to identify each of the following miracles of Jesus.

1. [brick wall] – I + [king] on the [C] (Matthew 14:25-27)

2. FIGHT - HT [tree] [bare tree] (Matthew 21:18-20)

3. [II] [cane] MEAN - A Kyŏŏrd (Matthew 21:18-20)

4. [girl's face] with [KLEENEX] - T of [1st plague pyramid] [shoe] (Luke 8:43-48)

5. [baseball glove and ball] of [fish] (Luke 5:4-9)

6. [water] (5th month) + d [goblet] (John 2:7-9)

REVELATION

A lot of Christians agree that the book of Revelation, the last book of the Bible, is difficult to understand. There are many different interpretations regarding the future events that are outlined within its pages, and there is no consensus as to which of these are correct. To many of us, it all seems so confusing that we wish to avoid this book altogether, especially from the fourth chapter onward. Seldom will you hear sermons preached from Revelation. However, the Lord considers this book to be very important. Did you know that Revelation is the only book of the Bible that promises a blessing upon those who read it (1:3)? Also, curses are pronounced upon anyone who either adds to or takes away from the words of the prophecy of the book (22:18–19).

We may not understand everything about Revelation, but one thing is certain. At its end is promised a fantastic future for God's people (chapters 21 and 22). No matter what happens in this life, nothing compares to the glories of heaven and eternal life with our precious Lord.

THE NEW JERUSALEM

What a glorious future awaits those who are Heaven bound! Indeed, a time will come when God will "wipe away all tears" (Revelation 21:4). When the frustrations and pressures of this life discourage you, consider the great joy that will be yours forever if Christ is your Savior. Also remember that the same God who holds your future is much in control of your present.

"Decode" the following words to reveal ten characteristics of the new Jerusalem promised by God. All the answers are found in Revelation. To help you "crack the code," the following example is given for you:

RIA NIVYWEPIQ
NEW JERUSALEM

1. AEXIV SJ PMJI (21:6)

_____

2. RIA LIEZIR ERH RIA IEVXL (21:1)

_____

3. PMKLX (21:11)

_____

4. XAIPZI KEXIW SJ TIEVP (21:21)

_____

5. XLVSRI SJ KSH (22:3)

_____

6. WXVIIXW SJ KSPH (21:21)

_____

7. RS RMKLX (22:5)

_____

8. XVII SJ PMJI (22:2)

_____

9. RS QSVI HIEXL (21:4)

_____

10. TVIGMSYW WXSRIW (21:19)

_____

65

PROMISES OF GOD

"I promise to do better."

"You can count on me."

"I will be there when you need me."

How often we hear promises from people that are broken. Some individuals mean well but forget what they promised. Others may be sincere at first, but changing circumstances or fear soon gets in the way. And others really have no intention of keeping their promises in the first place. In any case, it is discouraging when people do not follow through.

This is not so with God. We are told in 2 Corinthians 1:20 that all of His promises are assured. It is said that there are approximately seven thousand of them in the Bible! Here are listed just a few of God's promises from both the Old and New Testaments:

Strength—Isaiah 41:10, Philippians 4:13

Wisdom—Proverbs 3:5–6, James 1:5

Provision—Psalm 37:4–5, Philippians 4:19

Protection—Psalm 121:7–8, 2 Timothy 4:18

Peace—Isaiah 26:3, 1 Peter 5:7

Faithfulness—Lamentations 3:22–23, Hebrews 13:5

Help in temptation—Psalm 119:9 and11, Hebrews 2:18

Many of God's promises require something be done on our part in order to be activated. For instance, in Isaiah 26:3, God's peace is granted to those who set their minds on and trust in Him. But we can know for sure that the Lord will always do what He says. Read Joshua 23:14 and Numbers 23:19. People may break promises, but God never will. That is something you can always count on.

PROMISES FOR YOU

"Whereby are given unto us exceeding great and precious promises; that by these ye might be partakers of the divine nature" (2 Peter 1:4). How wonderful are God's promises to us! Yet most of them are not automatic. Obedience to His Word is essential in order to obtain them.

Given below are a few of God' many promises to us. But what must we do to obtain them? Look up the appropriate Scripture verses and write out what our part is.

1. If we _____ , He is faithful and just to forgive us our sins, and to cleanse us from all unrighteousness (1 John 1:9).
2. If we _____ , then we will not be judged (Matthew 7:1).
3. If we _____ , it shall be given unto us (Luke 6:38).
4. If we _____ , He will give us the desires of our hearts (Psalm 37:3, 4).
5. If we _____
   _____ , we will be fruitful, and whatever we do shall prosper (Psalm 1:2, 3).
6. If we _____
   _____ , He shall direct our paths (Proverbs 3:5, 6).
7. If we _____ , He will confess us before His Father in Heaven (Matthew 10:32).

8. If we _____ , we shall ask what we desire, and it will be done for us (John 15:7).
9. If we _____ _____ , He will keep us in perfect peace (Isaiah 26:3).
10. If we _____ , we will be able to stand against the wiles of the devil (Ephesians 6:11).
11. If we _____ _____ , the devil will flee from us (James 4: 7, 8).
12. If we _____ , we will not fulfill the lust of the flesh (Galatians 5:16).
13. If we _____ , He will sustain us and not allow us to be shaken (Psalm 55:22).
14. If we _____ _____ , we shall reap in due season (Galatians 6:9).
15. If we _____ , we will inherit His promises (Hebrews 6:12).

PURPOSE OF GOD

Many believers are familiar with Romans 8:28, which states that all things work together for good on behalf of those who love God and are called according to His purpose. But few know exactly what God's purpose for them is. This is revealed in the very next verse. Romans 8:29 declares that the Lord desires for us to be conformed to the image of His Son. That is, God wants us to be more like Jesus in our attitudes and actions.

This is not something that we can do on our own. Only as we surrender daily to the lordship of Christ and allow His Spirit to control us can we display true godly character. By faith, trust in God and allow Him to control your life. If you do this on a consistent basis, you will gradually become more like His beloved Son. God will be well pleased (Matthew 3:17).

JUST LIKE JESUS

A great desire of any Christian should be to grow in Christlikeness—to become more and more like Christ in word and in deed. As you work on this puzzle, you will discover many characteristics that Christlike people possess. The list may overwhelm you, but do not be discouraged. Pick out something specific and ask the Lord to help you manifest His life in that one area. If you are faithful in application, indeed the Lord *will* work in your life. The change will be wonderful to behold!

To solve this puzzle, first look up the verses and find the words that describe various elements of Christlikeness. The first letter of each answer is given for you. Then find and circle each word in the succeeding puzzle. The answers may be found across, down, diagonally, backwards, or forwards.

1. A _____ Romans 12:1
2. B _____ Proverbs 28:1
3. C _____ John 15:3
4. D _____ Luke 2:25
5. E _____ Ephesians 4:12
6. F _____ Revelation 2:10
7. G _____ Titus 3:2
8. H _____ Proverbs 16:19
9. I _____ 1 Peter 1:23
10. J _____ Psalm 35:9
11. K _____ Ephesians 4:32
12. L _____ 2 Samuel 1:23
13. M _____ 2 Peter 3:2

71

14. N _____ Acts 17:11
15. O _____ 2 Corinthians 2:9
16. P _____ Titus 1:15
17. Q _____ 1 Thessalonians 4:11
18. R _____ Proverbs 18:10
19. S _____ 1 Corinthians 15:58
20. T _____ 2 Corinthians 6:8
21. U _____ Psalm 119:1
22. V _____ 1 Peter 5:8
23. W _____ John 5:15
24. Y _____ Romans 6:19
25. Z _____ Revelation 3:19

I	M	I	N	D	F	U	L	E	Q	S	A	R
N	O	B	L	E	A	A	L	U	E	T	Z	U
C	R	A	D	V	O	B	I	X	L	E	E	N
O	N	C	S	O	M	E	R	T	O	A	A	D
R	K	T	I	U	T	O	B	Z	H	D	L	E
R	I	G	H	T	E	O	U	S	W	F	O	F
U	N	G	N	I	Y	F	I	D	E	A	U	I
P	D	E	D	L	E	I	Y	Y	U	S	S	L
T	Q	U	E	R	U	P	N	C	R	T	L	E
I	V	V	I	G	I	L	A	N	T	A	N	D
B	O	L	D	F	O	B	E	D	I	E	N	T
L	G	E	N	T	L	E	L	U	F	Y	O	J
E	L	B	A	T	P	E	C	C	A	R	B	Y

72

TEACHINGS OF CHRIST

Toward the end of each semester, college students have an opportunity to anonymously evaluate their courses and instructors. These are read after the semester is completed. I am encouraged in that my evaluations have been overwhelmingly positive. There has been occasional constructive criticism, and this has sometimes resulted in improvement in my teaching, for which I am grateful. In one case, however, I received a negative evaluation that had nothing to do with my teaching ability. It was simply a mean-spirited attack on my character. That hurt, but since I knew it was false, I rejected it. At the other extreme, I remember one day encountering a former student at the campus fitness center who said, "There goes the best professor at the university." I just rolled my eyes. *Oh, please …*

We should not be discouraged due to circumstances or the negative opinions of others. In the Beatitudes, Jesus explains how blessed his true followers are (Matthew 5:3–11). We are precious in His sight. On the other hand, we should not think too highly of ourselves. Jesus teaches us that those who exalt themselves will be humbled (Matthew 23:12).

It has been said that balance is the key to life. No matter what, good or bad, let us always desire to please God with a thankful and humble spirit.

"BE ATTITUDES"

Jesus' famous Beatitudes, from His Sermon on the Mount (Matthew 5), are aptly named. They represent *attitudes* of the heart that the Lord wants us to possess if we are to *be* like Him. These are more than mere words. All who actually live by them are promised abundant blessing.

Directions for this puzzle are as follows:

    (1) use the clues to determine each Beatitude along with each promise, and

    (2) match them up correctly by letter (one letter is used twice).

Beatitude:

1. opposite of rich / n i /   it (Verse 3) _____

2. before noon minus "ing" (Verse 4)

3. myself + k (Verse 5) _____

4. pyur / in / ♡ (Verse 8) _____

5. 👛 + e + good looking + d / 4 / not wrong + chus + Loch / Monster / 〰〰 — n (Verse 10) _____

6. i c r e m + opposite of empty (Verse 7) _____

74

7. nothing to eat / & / nothing to drink / opposite of

before / + eous + − t

(Verse 6) . _____

8. of cake + creators (Verse 9) _____

Promise:

A. C / HIM _____

B. motel + + it / the // our planet _____

C. head of state + m o d / ov / h + leaven − 1 _____

D. obtain / m = "verse" − v + e _____

E. B / com + 4 = Theodore (short for) _____

F. shouted after / the /// boys and girls / of / heavenly
   Father _____

G. B /abbreviation   for   Philippians + d

_____

Match by letter:

1. _____	5. _____
2. _____	6. _____
3. _____	7. _____
4. _____	8. _____

PARABLES OF JESUS

The most dangerous part of my commute is backing out of my own driveway. I live on a busy street where vehicles pass by quickly. A short distance to the north is a busy intersection, and I must always be aware of drivers not only passing straight through but making quick right or left turns. I must also check if cars or trucks are approaching from the south. A Catholic church stands directly across the street, where people occasionally exit the parking lot. Also, individuals could be passing by on foot or bicycle. I must always be patient and alert. Otherwise, it could spell disaster.

In the parable of the faithful steward (Luke 12:35–48), Jesus talks about two types of servants. Those going about their master's business want to be ready to meet their lord when he comes back, even if they do not know what time that will be. They remain steadfast and alert. Servants who believe his return is far off are not really concerned about the master and do whatever they please. They do not look for him. When the master returns, the former will be rewarded. The latter will suffer dire consequences.

Jesus will come at a time we do not expect (v. 46). We are exhorted to always be on the alert, wholeheartedly laboring for Him. If we remain faithful, our promised reward will be great.

PARABLE PUZZLE

A parable can be defined as a "simple story illustrating a profound moral or spiritual truth." Jesus' masterful use of parables invariably caught the attention of His listeners, as He sought to illustrate in simple terms what the kingdom of God is like. However, only those seeking true insight are really able to understand them. As Christ proclaims in Matthew 13:9, "Who hath ears to hear, let him hear."

Below you will find the names of fifteen well-known parables which are represented by awkward-sounding phrases. Write in the simplified names you are familiar with.

1. unfair magistrate _____ (Luke 18:1-8)

2. vicious farmers _____ (Matthew 21:33-45)

3. weights of money _____ (Matthew 25:14-30)

4. oyster gem of tremendous value _____ (Matthew 13:45, 46)

5. edible fruit tree in Israel _____ (Luke 21:29-32)

6. a dozen minus two chaste maidens _____ (Matthew 25:1-13)

7. dwelling erected on the stone _____ (Matthew 7:24-27)

77

8. yeast _____ (Matthew 13:33)

9. grain and the weeds _____ (Matthew 13:24-30, 36-43)

10. wasteful male offspring _____ (Luke 15:11-32)

11. hirelings at work in ground planted with cultivated grapevines _____ (Matthew 20:1-16)

12. misplaced piece of hard money _____ (Luke 15:8-10)

13. kind resident of the capitol of the Northern Kingdom _____ (Luke 10:30-37)

14. strayed wool-producing mammal _____ (Matthew 18:12-14)

15. seed scatter _____ (Matthew 13:1-9, 18-23)

CHRISTIAN FELLOWSHIP

I remember one day when I was at the dentist's office, a new dental assistant was asked to operate the x-ray machine. He asked, "Which way do you point this thing?" *Oh-oh* ...

On another occasion, I was giving a blood donation. When it was time to finish, a technician said, "What do I do now?" Yikes!

Initially, in neither case was I actually assured of a positive outcome. I certainly did not want to be damaged by x-rays or drained of all my blood. Fortunately, in each case, there was a skilled individual present who was able to guide the novice with respect to the proper procedure. I managed to get through both of these incidents unscathed.

Christians, especially those new to the faith, often wonder what to do or which way to turn. It is vitally important that other mature believers come alongside them to answer questions and help them grow spiritually. If you are a new believer, be sure to seek godly counsel. If you are a mature follower of Christ, invest yourself into others who may benefit from your wisdom and experience. God will be glorified.

FELLOW
BELIEVERS

"Behold, how good and how pleasant it is for brethren to dwell together in unity!" (Psalm 133:1) Do not neglect to gather together with others of the faith. Through them the Lord is able to encourage, strengthen, and guide you. Christians need each other.

Unscramble each of the following to spell out the names of New Testament believers. To help you, clues are provided.

1. HITS A MAT _____
2. A QUAIL _____
3. AS A BUG _____

4. ARMY _____
5. SUM NOISE _____
6. NABS A BAR _____

7. CORUS LINE _____
8. THE PENS _____

9. MY IT HOT _____
10. SOLO PAL _____

11. I'D A HOT SUPPER _____

12. BEE HOP _____

13. LASSI _____

14. O HE'L PUSH IT _____
15. CARS DO _____

Clues:

1. chosen to replace Judas
2. Priscilla's husband
3. prophesied concerning Paul's journey to Jerusalem
4. seven devils cast out of her
5. former slave of Philemon
6. disputed with Paul concerning John Mark
7. sent to Joppa for Peter
8. served tables; full of faith and power
9. mother a Jew, father a Greek
10. new believer mighty in the Scriptures
11. sent by Paul to the Philippians
12. a sister commended by Paul to the Romans
13. locked up in a Philippian jail with Paul
14. written to by Luke
15. raised from the dead through Peter

PRAYERS

There are many verses in the Bible that have to do with prayer. One of the most often quoted is found in Philippians 4:6–7. Here we are instructed not to worry about anything but rather to pray to God about our concerns. As a result, we believe His supernatural peace through Jesus is assured. However, within this passage tucked inside are two words that are often overlooked. These words are "with thanksgiving."

I don't know about you, but when something goes wrong, my first reaction is to complain about it. If a computer glitch suddenly happens, I begin to worry. If I am interrupted, I far too often (at least inwardly) get upset. If I cannot find something I misplaced, I get frustrated. I suppose this is natural for most people. But when I have taken the time to calm down and pray with thanksgiving, it's made a big difference. I would say something like "OK, Lord. You know where I misplaced my eyeglasses, and I thank you for showing me exactly where they are." I don't know how many times I have taken this approach, and God answered my prayer. Needless to say, I am a work in progress and still grumble far too often. But the Lord is gracious. It is amazing what He does if I only stop to give Him thanks.

No matter what your problem happens to be, large or small, take a deep breath, relax, and thank Him for the answer even before you receive it. Your prayer may be answered quickly. Or you will be granted His peace, knowing He is in control and will eventually work things out for your good (Romans 8:28). You cannot lose when you give God thanks.

FAMOUS PRAY-ERS

"The effectual fervent prayer of a righteous man availeth much" (James 5:16). God really answers prayer. Yet few people actually take the time to pray to the Lord, expecting to receive results. Reflect on your own prayer life (or lack of one) as you consider the individuals below who prayed. Remember, you "have not" if you "ask not."

Match each well-known prayer (Column 2) with the person(s) who prayed (Column 1).

Column 1	Column 2
1. _____ Abraham (Genesis 18:20-32)	A. proof of his call
2. _____ Christians (Acts 12:5)	B. Peter (while in prison)
3. _____ Daniel (Daniel 9:16-19)	C. wisdom in ruling the people
4. _____ David (Psalm 51:1-19)	D. death
5. _____ Elijah (James 5:17, 18)	E. health
6. _____ Elijah (1 Kings 19:1-4)	F. the Jewish people in captivity
7. _____ Gideon (Judges 6:36-40)	G. relief for Pharaoh
8. _____ Hannah (1 Samuel 1:9-18)	H. personal repentance
9. _____ Hezekiah (2 Kings 20:11)	I. physical strength
10. _____ Jabez (1 Chronicles 4:10)	J. spiritual strength and love
11. _____ Jesus (John 17:20-23)	K. a son
12. _____ Moses (Exodus 8:29-31)	L. prosperity
13. _____ Paul (Ephesians 3:14-21)	M. unity for all believers
14. _____ Samson (Judges 16:28-30)	N. Sodom
15. _____ Solomon (1 Kings 3:5-10)	O. rain

HEAVEN

There have been recent changes in my job. After being used to teaching in the classroom, I have to learn how to teach remotely—that is, perform what is called distance learning. This requires adjusting to new technology, something I am not good at. I am fortunate to have received outside help, but I am a slow learner in this area, and it is frustrating when I forget things and make mistakes. All of us, even if we love our jobs, go through those times when things seem to fall apart. For those who don't like their work in the first place, it may be tempting to give up or just walk away.

But work is ordained of God. Jesus declared in John 5:17 (NASB), "My Father is working until now, and I Myself am working." If the Lord is working, it is logical to assume that His people were created to work as well. Indeed, Adam, the first man, was given the responsibility of cultivating the land (Genesis 2:15).

You might be interested to know that believers' work does not cease here. There will be work to do in heaven as well. Some of you might think, *No! This sounds more like a curse than a blessing!* But stop and consider this: in heaven, there will be no curse (Revelation 22:3). Remember the parable of the ten talents? "His lord said to him, 'well done, good and faithful servant, you were faithful over a few things, I will make you ruler over many things. Enter into the joy of your lord'" (Matthew 25:21 NKJV). What exactly we will do in heaven is uncertain. But we know that whatever work we perform, it will be most satisfying. In heaven, there will be everlasting joy.

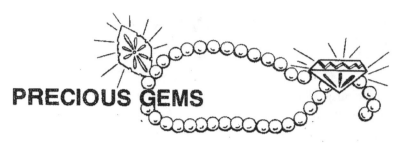

PRECIOUS GEMS

Earthly riches are very attractive, but true riches are found only in Heaven. "Lay not up for yourselves treasures upon earth ... but lay up for yourselves treasures in heaven" declared Jesus. "For where your treasure is, there will your heart be also" (Matthew 6:19-21).

Circle the names of fourteen different precious stones in the puzzle below. You will find them either across, down, diagonally, backwards, or forwards. The uncircled letters (when read down from left to right) spell out what our attitude toward earthly riches should be. (Check Revelation 21:19, 20; Proverbs 8:11; Jeremiah 17:1; Ezekiel 27:16; and Revelation 22:1 if you need help.)

J	A	S	P	E	R	P	D	U	D
T	M	G	Y	B	U	R	I	L	T
H	E	E	A	K	I	J	A	X	C
N	T	G	D	T	A	R	M	Y	R
C	H	A	L	C	E	D	O	N	Y
O	Y	M	I	M	T	O	N	O	S
F	S	N	E	G	O	O	D	D	T
D	T	L	Y	R	E	B	P	R	A
H	F	I	R	S	C	O	R	A	L
T	E	R	I	H	P	P	A	S	Z

Letters spell out: _____

STRANGE THINGS

Back in the early 1960s, during the early days of space travel, space scientists began investigating the trajectories of the sun, moon, and planets along with known asteroids and meteors. The purpose of this was to assure safe satellite orbits in preparation for the coming moon landing. There is an interesting story (later denied by NASA officials) that, as computerized statistical measurements were performed back and forth over the centuries, the computer showed that there was an entire twenty-four-hour day missing in elapsed time. The scientists were puzzled. They could not find any logical explanation for this. Then someone suggested that they check out a very interesting passage in the book of Joshua. According to Joshua 10:7–13, while battling the kings of the Amorites, Joshua prayed for the sun to stand still, and God granted his request. The sun did not go down for about a whole day. Sure enough, by checking with the computer, the scientists discovered that during Joshua's time, there was a time lapse of twenty-three hours and twenty minutes or, as the Bible says, *about a whole day*. However, there were still forty minutes not accounted for. The scientists were then directed to another unusual biblical account, this time from 2 Kings 20:9–11. Ailing King Hezekiah asked God for a sign that He would heal him. Through the prophet Isaiah, as proof of this, the Lord caused the shadow on a sundial to move backward ten degrees. The sun travels around the earth 360 degrees in one day. This calculates to $\frac{360 \; deg}{1 \; day} \times \frac{1 \; day}{24 \; hrs} \times \frac{1 \; hr}{60 \; min} = \frac{1}{4}$ degree per minute. Forty minutes, the remaining missing time according to the scientists' computer, is exactly $\frac{1}{4}$ x 40 = 10 degrees, which perfectly matches the biblical account. It is interesting to note that around 701 BC (when Hezekiah was king of Judah), new calendars introducing the 365-day year were introduced, replacing the 360-day biblical year. Something very unusual must have happened to initiate such a drastic change.

True believers should not be surprised. The Creator of all things can alter His natural order any way He wishes. No matter how strange a Bible passage appears to be, we can trust it to be true.

MOST
UNUSUAL—
BUT TRUE

Despite claims that the Bible is a dull book, it is on the contrary filled with many interesting and unusual accounts. It is said that "truth is stranger than fiction," and this is certainly the case regarding Scripture. No matter how strange or impossible the following situations seem to be, you are assured that they actually occurred—because God said they did.

How many of the following "unusual things" from the Bible do you remember? Fill in your answers in the blanks provided.

    1. John the Baptist ate _____ and _____ for food (Matthew 3:4).
    2. Hezekiah lived _____ extra years because he prayed (Isaiah 38:1-5).
    3. Because of Elisha, the _____ _____ floated in the water (2 Kings 6:1-6).
    4. The _____ stood still for almost a whole day, so Joshua and the Israelites could win the battle (Joshua 10:13).
    5. There once lived a giant who had _____ fingers on each hand and _____ toes on each foot (2 Samuel 21:20).
    6. Jacob once used _____ for a pillow (Genesis 28:10, 11).
    7. Paul was bitten by a _____ but was unhurt, and he merely shook it into the fire (Acts 28:3-6).

8. Through Ezekiel's vision, a valley of _____ _____ was resurrected to life (Ezekiel 37:1-10).

9. Og king of Bashan had a _____ thirteen and one-half feet long and six feet wide (1 cubit = 1½ feet; Deuteronomy 3:11).

10. King _____ had seven hundred wives and they led his heart astray (1 Kings 11:2, 3).

11. _____ the prophet walked naked for three years (Isaiah 20:2, 3).

12. Captive women, according to the laws of ancient Israel, had to _____ their heads before they could marry (Deuteronomy 21:10-13).

13. When the tribe of Benjamin rebelled against Israel, included among their numbers was a chosen army of seven hundred men who were _____ - _____ (Judges 20:15, 16).

14. The sun travelled _____ for Hezekiah (Isaiah 38:8).

15. A battle was won because _____ hands were just held up (Exodus 17:11-13).

BIBLE MINISTRIES AND OCCUPATIONS

I remember the very first job I ever had. I was a summer day camp counselor during my late teens. It didn't pay much, but I liked kids and loved to make them laugh. It was a joy to serve them through many fun activities, including various games, sporting events, arts and crafts, swimming, and field trips. Contests held every other Friday morning were very popular because a member of each winning team got to smash a whipped cream pie in a counselor's face! When I first started working, I didn't know that getting pied would be part of my job, but I did hope to make kids laugh. Well, I certainly got what I wished for.

Later, I taught math to middle school, high school, and eventually college students. By thorough class preparation, impartial grading, and patiently explaining math concepts, my goal has always been to serve my students and help them succeed in their studies. I like to see them laugh as well. For instance, in math,

$\sqrt{}$ is a giant square root symbol (root bar), $\sqrt{}$ a medium-sized root bar, and $\sqrt{}$ a baby root bar. (Get it? Baby Ruth bar. Candy). Ha.

Throughout the years, I've enjoyed favor and good success working with young people. However, sometimes I've wondered about my motivation. Is my desire to serve them and make them laugh meant to honor God? Or is it only to please them or make myself look good? Motive is sometimes difficult to determine. We are definitely commanded to serve others, but Paul exhorts us that whatever we do, do it as unto the Lord and not unto men (2 Corinthians 4:5, Colossians 3:23). God encourages us to let Him search our hearts (Psalm 139:23–24) in order to reveal our true motives and allow Him to guide us along His paths for His glory. This is good advice no matter what our occupations happen to be.

WORK FOR THE LORD

Have you ever thought about the type of occupation you'd like to have in the future? Often this is a difficult decision to make. Ask the Lord to guide you, and He is sure to do so. Contrary to what many believe, what God has in store for you will be something you'll like, and something for which you will be well suited. The Lord uses people in all types of jobs when they are yielded to Him.

Each description of our Lord given below will remind you of a certain occupation. From the list at the end of the puzzle, choose which *best* fits in each case.

Occupations to choose from:

1. bread of life (John 6:35) _____ ambassador
2. Lord of the harvest (Luke 10:2) _____ architect
3. good master (Matthew 23:8) _____ astronomer
4. chief cornerstone (1 Peter 2:6) _____ baker
5. great teacher (Rabbi) (John 3:2) _____ banker
6. tidings of great joy (Luke 2:10) _____ builder
7. Sun of righteousness (Malachi 4:2) _____ carpenter
8. Rock of ages (1 Corinthians 10:4) _____ doctor
9. captain of the Lord's host (Joshua 5:15) _____ educator
10. hidden treasure (Matthew 13:44) _____ farmer
11. desire of all nations (Haggai 2:7) _____ florist
12. great physician (Luke 4:23) _____ geologist
13. sure foundation (Isaiah 28:16) _____ jeweler
14. pearl of great price (Matthew 13:45, 46) _____ lawyer
15. door (John 10:9) _____ musician
16. Counselor (Isaiah 9:6) _____ newspaperman
17. rose of Sharon (Song of Solomon 2:1) _____ philosopher
18. Prince of Peace (Isaiah 9:6) _____ servant
19. a new song (Revelation 5:9) _____ soldier
20. wisdom of God (1 Corinthians 1:24) _____ statesman

BIBLE WOMEN

My father was a very organized person. He was so organized that paper clips in his desk drawer were all parallel. Sometimes his organizing exasperated my mother. She was a professional artist, and one day, with nothing better to do, Dad decided to "help her out" by rearranging her paints in alphabetical order. Needless to say, that did not go over well at all.

If you read Luke 10:38–42, you will learn about a woman named Martha who also appeared to be well organized. She was making preparations for Jesus's visit and wanted to make sure everything was right, all the details covered. She was upset with her sister Mary who, instead of helping her, sat at the feet of Jesus, listening to Him. Jesus reminded Martha of what was most important—seeking the Lord.

This does not mean that organized preparation is wrong. At times, it is appropriate. But the Lord is saying that some of us have a tendency to fret over details unnecessarily, often at the expense of spending quality time with Him. Read Ecclesiastes 2:10–11. Make God the first priority in your life (Matthew 6:33), and everything else will fall into its proper place.

FAMOUS BIBLE WOMEN

Godly women provide great blessing for all those around them. On the other hand, ungodly women may cause considerable strife. (The same goes for men as well!) Consider the character of the following Bible women, and how others were affected by their actions. Whether we know it or not, *others are affected* by what we do—whether it be good or bad.

Unscramble letters in each problem below to give the names of famous Bible women. A clue is given to each (but not in order).

1. HEAL _____
   (Genesis 29:21-23)
2. A TRAM _____
   (Genesis 38:6)
3. HIS VAT _____
   (Esther 1:19)
4. BAD HERO _____
   (Judges 4:4)
5. MYRA _____
   (Luke 1:30, 31)
6. LEARCH _____
   (Genesis 29:28-30)
7. HER BEAK _____
   (Genesis 24:67)
8. CLAIM H _____
   (1 Samuel 18:20, 21)
9. I HEAL BEST _____
   (Luke 1:57-60)
10. SHEAR _____
    (Genesis 46:17)
11. HABITAT _____
    (Acts 9:40)
12. HURT _____
    (Ruth 4:13-22)

a. daughter-in-law of Judah

b. judge of Israel

c. raised from the dead by Peter

d. mother of John the Baptist

e. great-grandmother of David

f. daughter of Asher

g. wife of David

h. wife of Isaac

i. first wife of Jacob

j. mother of Jesus

k. queen succeeded by Esther

l. favorite wife of Jacob

BIBLE NUMBERS

There has been much speculation as to the validity of the last few verses of the Gospel of Mark. Some believe that verses 9–20 of chapter 16 should not be part of scripture because they are omitted from some of the oldest manuscripts. A careful study of the Greek text, however, yields some startling results:

- number of words: 175 = 7 x 25
- number of vocabulary words: 98 = 7 x 14
- number of letters: 553 = 7 x 79
- number of vowels: 294 = 7 x 42
- number of consonants: 259 = 7 x 37
- number of forms: 133 = 7 x 19
- number of forms that occur once: 112 = 7 x 16
- number of forms that occur more than once: 21 = 7 x 3
- number of vocabulary words spoken by Jesus: 42 = 7 x 6
- number of vocabulary words not spoken: 56 = 7 x 8

There are three divisions of this passage: Jesus's appearance to Mary Magdalene (verses 9–11, 35 = 7 x 5 words); Jesus's appearance to the disciples (verses 12–18, 105 = 7 x 15 words); and Jesus's ascension (verses 19–20, 35 = 7 x 5 words).

All of this is most remarkable. If you believe these patterns of sevens occur by pure chance, try to compose your own passage of the same length in any subject in English or any other language subject to the criteria above. Your chance of success is practically zero. This presents strong evidence that Mark 16:9–20 is part of God's Word, which is saturated with the number seven.

BIBLE NUMBERS QUIZ

Numbers often play an important role in the Bible. Through them God reveals to us a part of His nature. He is not removed from His creation. He is a specific God who is very concerned with specific details. He knows all things and even the "little things" in our lives are important to Him.

See how many Bible numbers you can remember by answering the following:

1. The oldest man in the Bible lived _____ years (Genesis 5:27).
2. Peter caught _____ fish in his net (John 21:11).
3. Jesus chose _____ disciples (Matthew 10:1).
4. To the Lord one day is as _____ years (2 Peter 3:8).
5. Jesus fed _____ men with five loaves and two fish (Matthew 14:19-21).
6. At the time of the great flood, it rained _____ days and _____ nights (Genesis 7:12).
7. When he was old, the apostle John wrote to _____ churches in Asia (Revelation 1:4).
8. There were _____ disciples in the upper room on the Day of Pentecost (Acts 1:15; 2:1).
9. The number of the beast is _____ (Revelation 13:18).
10. An angel of the Lord killed _____ Assyrians in one night (2 Kings 19:35).
11. Rehoboam was the father to a total of _____ children (2 Chronicles 11:21).
12. Gideon's army numbered _____ men (Judges 7:6, 7).
13. Around the throne in Heaven sat _____ elders (Revelation 4:4).
14. On Mount Zion stood a Lamb with _____ having His Father's name written on their foreheads (Revelation 14:1).
15. The boy Jesus remained at the temple in Jerusalem when He was _____ years old (Luke 2:42, 43).

MORE BIBLE NUMBERS

Three is said to be the number of divine perfection or completeness. This is demonstrated frequently throughout scripture. Of course, God the Father, God the Son, and God the Holy Spirit (the Trinity) comes to mind. In John 14:6, Jesus tells us He is the way, the truth, and the life. In Revelation, we read, "Holy, holy, holy, Lord God Almighty, who was and is and is to come" (Revelation 4:8 NKJV). Notice the patterns of threes. In reference to Jesus, we know the following:

- *Three times* He was spoken to by a voice from heaven.
- He endured a *threefold* temptation in the wilderness.
- He raised *three* people from the dead: a widow's son at Nain (Luke 7:11–16), Jairus's daughter (Mark 5:35–43), and Lazarus (John 11:43–44).
- He was crucified on the *third* hour.
- There were *three* hours of darkness while He was on the cross.
- On the *third* day, He was raised from the dead.

God displays perfection and completeness through other numerical patterns as well. Seven is the number of spiritual perfection. Ten is the number of ordinal perfection. Twelve is the number of governmental perfection.

In Philippians 1:6, we are told that He who has begun a good work in us will perfect and complete it until the day of Jesus Christ's return. What a comfort it is to know that the God of completeness so cares about each of us. He is always at work in us, both to will and to do of His good pleasure (Philippians 2:13). Let us worship and praise Him.

FIRST THINGS

"And he is before all things, and by him all things consist: and he is the head of the body, the church: who is the begining, the firstborn from the dead; that in all things he might have the preeminence" (Colossians 1:17, 18). Christ is indeed first in all things, whether people believe it or not. Give Him the honor and glory He so richly deserves.

Answer each of the following by circling the letter of the correct answer. All refer to "first things" as mentioned in the Bible.

1. Who was the first Hebrew? (Genesis 14:13)
   A. Adam   C. Abraham
   B. Seth   D. David
2. According to John's Gospel (John 1:35-40), the first of the twelve disciples to come to know Jesus was
   A. Andrew   C. James
   B. Peter   D. John
3. Israel's first king (1 Samuel 10:17-25) was
   A. David   C. Saul
   B. Samuel   D. Hezekiah
4. The first recorded prophecy (Genesis 3:15) was given by
   A. the Lord to Abraham
   B. Abraham to Lot
   C. Moses to the Egyptians
   D. the Lord to the serpent in Eden
5. What was the first miracle of Jesus? (John 2:1-11)
   A. He fed 5000 men with five loaves and two fish.
   B. He turned water into wine.
   C. He healed a man born blind.
   D. He delivered a boy oppressed by evil spirits.

6. Who was the first shepherd? (Genesis 4:2)
   A. Seth   C. Adam
   B. David   D. Abel
7. When Paul began his first missionary journey, where did he sail first? (Acts 13:2-4)
   A. Cyprus   C. Antioch
   B. Jerusalem   D. Rome
8. The first person to see Jesus after He rose from the dead Mark 16:9) was
   A. Peter   C. Mary Magdalene
   B. John   D. Cleopas
9. The first recorded war (Genesis 14:1-12) involved kings from each of the following places with the exception of
   A. Gomorrah   C. Sodom
   B. Moab   D. Elam
10. The first rainbow (Genesis 9:14, 15) occurred in connection with
   A. the creation of the land and seas
   B. the crossing of the Red Sea
   C. the sacrifice of Isaac
   D. the termination of the great flood
11. The first disciple to confess Jesus as the Son of God (John 1:47-49) was
   A. Peter   C. John
   B. Nathanael   D. Judas
12. The first person known to have built an altar of sacrifice (Genesis 8:20) to God was
   A. Noah   C. Adam
   B. Moses   D. David

ANIMALS AND INSECTS

I will not let You go unless You bless me.
—Genesis 32:26 (NKJV)

Early one afternoon, while preparing for a meal, I wished to remove some food from my refrigerator. However, I first had to check the whereabouts of my two cats, Tabitha and Barnabas. One was down in the basement, and the other was sleeping upstairs in my bedroom. Perfect. The coast was clear. I ever so quietly opened the refrigerator door, removed some lunchmeat, and tiptoed toward the kitchen counter. But before I even got there, both cats immediately appeared, one on my right and one on my left, expecting handouts. I could not believe it! Of course I had to share with both of them part of my lunch.

When my cats rushed to my side, they fully expected to receive something good from me. You could say they were tuned in to a blessing and knew that I would provide it. There is a lesson here that we can all learn from. Far too often, we forfeit God's blessing in our lives. Why might this be so? Some people think they know themselves what is best and refuse God's blessing. Others fail to patiently wait for God's timing and settle for less, sometimes far less, than what the Lord intended to give them. And others simply believe they are not worthy to be blessed. The latter are actually right because nobody deserves anything good from God (Romans 3:23). But that is not the point. God chooses to bless us because He is by nature so merciful and generous. "If you then, being evil, know how to give good gifts to your children, how much more will your Father who is in heaven give good things to those who ask Him" (Matthew 7:11 NKJV). Still others, being distracted by worldly pursuits, never look for God's blessing at all.

How my cats knew to run to my side when food came out I'll never know. But they were not distracted. They pursued the blessing. You can do the same. Expect God to bless you, not because you deserve it but because He loves you. You never know what good things may come your way.

 # ANIMAL

BACKERS

One of the reasons why people like animals so much is because they are loyal and trusting. Your dog or cat doesn't judge you or eye you with suspicion. He just loves you for whom you are. How the Lord desires this type of attitude in us. Jesus described Nathanael as "an Israelite indeed, in whom is no guile" (John 1:47). Is this how He would describe you?

The following Scriptures, by way of comparison, make reference to animals. Fill in the blanks with the correct names. (Answers to choose from are given.)

1. "Now shall this company lick up all that are round about us, as the _____ licketh up the grass of the field" (Numbers 22:4).
2. "And the Philistine said unto David, Am I a _____, that thou comest to me with staves?" (1 Samuel 17:43)
3. "They that wait upon the Lord shall renew their strength; they shall mount up with wings as _____" (Isaiah 40:31).
4. "Can the Ethiopian change his skin, or the _____ his spots? Then may ye also do good, that are accustomed to do evil" (Jeremiah 13:23).
5. "But unto you that fear my name shall the sun of righteousness arise with healing in his wings; and ye shall go forth, and grow up as _____ of the stall" (Malachi 4:2).
6. "Behold, I send you forth as _____ in the midst of _____" (Matthew 10:16).

7. "Be ye therefore wise as _____ , and harmless as _____ " (Matthew 10:16).

8. "Ye blind guides, which strain at a gnat, and swallow a _____ " (Matthew 23:24).

9. "He shall separate them one from another, as a shepherd divideth his sheep from the _____ " (Matthew 25:32).

10. "And he said unto them, Go ye, and tell that _____ . Behold, I cast out devils, and I do cures today and tomorrow" (Luke 13:32).

11. "Behold, the _____ of God, which taketh away the sin of the world" (John 1:29).

12. "Your adversary the devil, as a roaring _____ , walketh about, seeking whom he may devour" (1 Peter 5:8).

13. "And the shapes of the locusts were like unto _____ prepared unto battle" (Revelation 9:7).

Answers to choose from:

calves	fox	lion
camel	goats	ox
dog	horses	serpents
doves	Lamb	sheep
eagles	leopard	wolves

INSECT INSPECTION

Insects, though small in size, can be very irritating. In this way they are analogous to life in general. Small grievances, petty annoyances, little irritations—all take their toll. Often it's in little things where the devil trips us up. Keep your mind set on the Lord, and don't allow the little things to upset you. "Nay, in all these things we are more than conquerors through him that loved us" (Romans 8:37).

In the puzzle below, circle the names of fourteen different insects found in the Bible. They are arranged forwards, backwards, across, down, or diagonally. Here are some verses to help you: Psalm 78:46; Isaiah 50:9; Numbers 13:33; Exodus 8:21; 1 Samuel 24:14; Micah 7:17, Exodus 8:16; Proverbs 30:28; Exodus 10:4; Proverbs 6:6; Leviticus 11:22; Matthew 23:24; Deuteronomy 7:20; Judges 14:8

```
R  A  L  L  I  P  R  E  T  A  C
M  O  T  H  N  O  T  B  A  B  O
N  E  C  T  O  H  U  L  E  E  D
G  R  A  S  S  H  O  P  P  E  R
B  E  F  U  F  L  Y  R  T  T  G
O  U  N  C  A  E  L  F  N  L  N
D  M  R  O  W  H  T  R  A  E  A
E  C  I  L  S  P  I  D  E  R  T
```

After you have circled all of your answers, the remaining letters spell out the result of God's protection of His people during the Egyptian plagues. Swarms of flies covered Egypt, but in Goshen _____ .

MOUNTAINS

Read Matthew 17:2–21. Most believers are familiar with the incident where Jesus led Peter, James, and John up a high mountain and was transfigured before them. Moses and Elijah appeared and talked with Jesus, and Peter remarked how good it was to be there. He even wanted to set up shelters for them. However, they could not stay. When they came down, the situation was quite different. In contrast to the glory at the mountaintop, down below they had to deal with a demonic spirit.

All of us experience highs and lows. It is a part of life. But we need to remember that no matter what our circumstances, God is always with us. Jesus is the same yesterday, today, and forever (Hebrews 13:8). Whether at the top of the mountain or the bottom of the valley, the Lord has everything in control and will never leave or forsake you (in the Old Testament, Deuteronomy 31:6, repeated in the New Testament, Hebrews 13:5). Always trust in Him.

NAME THAT MOUNTAIN

It is through "mountaintop" experiences that we as Christians often come into close contact with the Lord, and gain the strength we need to face life's problems. Important things indeed seem to take place atop mountains, both spiritually and in many other ways. The Bible clearly indicates this through the following examples.

Match by letter the correct name of the mountain where each of the following Biblical events took place:

1. _____ Moses viewed the promised land (Deuteronomy 34:1)   A. Sinai

2. _____ King Saul died (1 Samuel 31:8)   B. Gilead

3. _____ Abraham offered Isaac as a sacrifice (Genesis 22:1, 2)   C. Moriah

4. _____ David captured it (2 Samuel 5:7)   D. Carmel

5. _____ Laban overtook Jacob (Genesis 31:20-25)   E. Ararat

6. _____ God gave the law through Moses (Exodus 19:2-7)   F. Nebo

7. _____ Jesus spoke of the future (Matthew 24:3)   G. Olives

8. _____ Esau and his descendents lived here (Deuteronomy 2:1-5)   H. Gilboa

9. _____ After the flood, the ark rested here (Genesis 8:4)   I. Zion

10. _____ Elijah challenged the prophets of Baal (1 Kings 18:17-19)   J. Seir

PLANTS, TREES, SHRUBS

A rock garden exists in my backyard. It is obviously low maintenance, but there is one difficulty I occasionally have to cope with. Anyone who tends a lawn or garden knows exactly what that problem is—the presence of weeds. They seem to grow so effortlessly, but it takes a lot of time-consuming work to pluck them out. If the roots are not pulled up, the issue is not resolved, and usually such weeds quickly grow back.

Scripture alludes to this in Hebrews 12:15. Here we are told that roots of bitterness springing up cause much trouble, defiling many. As weeds easily pop up, how quickly some people take offense. Just as a garden looks good for a while if only the surface weeds are removed, many individuals may appear fine outwardly when they deal with their bitter feelings only at a shallow level. However, if the root cause of one's bitterness is not discerned and dealt with, its deadly effects sooner or later spring up.

Victory is promised in surrendered lives (2 Corinthians 2:14), but there are times when we must allow the Master Gardener to uproot what is necessary in order to achieve it. It is not a quick or easy process, but lasting freedom will result.

TREE STUMPERS

Trees are invariably associated with life. The "tree of life" in Genesis 2, the "tree planted by the rivers of water" in Psalm 1, and the tree "for the healing of the nations" in Revelation 22 are all representative examples. If we delight in the Lord and meditate on his Word, we will, like trees, flourish and bear good fruit. (See Psalm 1:2, 3.)

In the lettergram below, circle the names of fifteen trees found in the Bible. Answers may appear forward or backward, in either a row, a column, or a diagonal.

C	E	D	A	R	Y	A	M	P
H	L	L	N	A	V	L	O	O
E	T	R	I	F	C	P	O	M
S	R	G	O	P	L	D	L	E
T	Y	I	B	A	I	L	I	G
N	M	F	R	L	D	N	V	R
U	E	L	M	M	X	H	E	A
T	W	O	L	L	I	W	G	N
S	Y	C	A	M	O	R	E	A
T	R	U	S	K	A	P	Z	T
S	S	E	R	P	Y	C	B	E

ANSWERS

The Character of God:

1. Love
2. Light
3. A consuming fire
4. A Spirit
5. The Word
6. Infinite
7. Eternal
8. All-powerful
9. Everywhere present
10. All-knowing
11. Most High God
12. Lord God
13. God Almighty
14. I Am
15. Holy One of Israel
16. Heavenly Father
17. Jesus
18. The world
19. Pride, lying, shedding of innocent blood, wicked planning, eagerness to do evil, false testimony, sowing discord among brothers
20. Loving-kindness, justice, righteousness

"I AM":

1. Light of the world
2. Bread of life
3. Alpha and Omega, or first and last, or beginning and end
4. Door

5. Good Shepherd
6. Way, truth, and life
7. Root and offspring of David
8. True vine
9. Bright and morning star
10. Jesus
11. "I AM"

The Many Names of Christ:

1. Daniel
2. Hebrews
3. Revelation
4. Jeremiah
5. Joshua
6. 1 Peter
7. Psalms
8. John
9. Isaiah
10. Song of Solomon
11. Genesis
12. Matthew
13. Luke
14. Numbers
15. Malachi

Ark Work:

Across:

3. Animals
5. Shem
6. Eight
8. Pitch
10. Water

13. Rainbow
14. God
16. Olive

Down:

1. Three
2. Japheth
4. Noah
7. Gopher
9. Ham
11. Raven
12. Forty
15. Dove

The Hall of Faith:

1. Offered a more excellent sacrifice
2. Pleased God
3. Prepared an ark to the saving of his house
4. Delivered a child when past age
5. Offered up Isaac
6. Blessed Jacob and Esau concerning things to come
7. Blessed both sons of Joseph
8. Gave commandment concerning his bones
9. Kept the Passover
10. Received the spies

Joseph: Up from the Depths:

1. Jacob
2. On
3. Coat
4. Simeon
5. Asenath

6. Ephraim
7. Benjamin
8. Potiphar
9. Egypt
10. Dreams
11. Hebrews
12. Rachel
13. Prison
14. Baker
15. Ears

The Ten Plagues:

1. Boils-6
2. Frogs-2
3. Hail-7
4. Darkness-9
5. River turned into blood-1
6. Locusts-8
7. Murrain (cattle) died-5
8. Flies-4
9. Death of the firstborn-10
10. Lice (gnats)-3

Letters spelled out: The Lord God

Total Obedience:

1. Peter
2. Noah
3. Matthew
4. Isaiah
5. Paul
6. Joshua
7. Abram

8. Hezekiah
9. David
10. Philip
11. Elijah
12. Daniel
13. Caleb
14. Moses

Judge for Yourself:

Across:

1. Gideon
4. Othniel
10. Barak
11. Deborah
12. Shamgar
13. Samuel
15. Eli
16. Samson

Down:

2. Elon
3. Jephthah
5. Tola
6. Ehud
7. Jair
8. Ibzan
9. Abimelech
14. Abdon

Heart Exam:

Across: murmurings, envy, fear, murder, blasphemy

Down: hypocrisy, strife, pride, idolatry, rebellion

Diagonal: lust, hate, deceit, bitterness

Letters spelled out: Think on good things

A Royal Problem:

Across:

2. Nadab
5. Jeroboam
8. Shallum
10. Ahab
11. Zimri
13. Hoshea
14. Jehu
15. Ahaziah

Down:

1. Rehoboam
3. Asa
4. Jehoshaphat
6. Hezekiah
7. Manasseh
9. Uzziah
12. Ahaz
14. Joash

Wait on the Lord:

1. C
2. F
3. H
4. G
5. D
6. B
7. E
8. I
9. A
10. J

Young and Old Alike:

1. J
2. F
3. K
4. L
5. C
6. N
7. D
8. H
9. O
10. G
11. A
12. E
13. B
14. I
15. M

Our Unseen World:

1. The devil as a roaring lion, walks about, seeking whom he may devour.
2. The Lord fills heaven and earth.
3. The Spirit of God dwells in you.
4. Where two or three are gathered together in Jesus's name, He is in their midst.
5. We wrestle against spiritual rulers of darkness in high places.
6. Angels minister for them who are heirs of salvation.
7. We are surrounded by a great cloud of witnesses.
8. In hell, the worm never dies, and the fire is never quenched.
9. Jesus is set down at the right hand of the throne of God.
10. The Lord sits upon the circle of the earth.

Stepping through Psalms:

1. 23:1
2. 150:6
3. 119
4. 37:3
5. 90
6. 24:10
7. 139:23
8. 122.6
9. 1:2
10. 117
11. 16:10
12. 34:7
13. 51:10
14. 100:4

A book of praises

A Walk through Proverbs:

1. Solomon
2. To give us wisdom and understanding
3. God allows them to eat the fruit of their own way.
4. He will fully meet our needs; we will have abundance.
5. A person who sows discord among brothers
6. The scorner will hate you for it; the wise man will love you for it.
7. Without counsel there is defeat; with many counselors there is victory.
8. Death
9. Soft, gentle answers
10. Friends are separated
11. Death and life are in the power of the tongue.
12. Their hearts are in His hand; as rivers of water, He can turn them any way He wishes.
13. When they are older, they will not depart from it.
14. As a person thinks in his heart, so is he.
15. They perish.
16. She will be greatly praised.

Prophecy Fulfilled:

1. O-C
2. G-J
3. F-B
4. J-L
5. C-E
6. Q-A
7. A-N
8. H-G
9. M-Q
10. I-K
11. B-F
12. E-O
13. K-I

14. D-P
15. P-H
16. N-M
17. L-D

Miracles of Old:

1. Moses at the burning bush
2. fire falling from heaven at the call of Elijah
3. the three Hebrew men delivered from the fiery furnace
4. Mount Sinai as it appeared to the children of Israel when the Lord descended upon it
5. creation of the animals
6. donkey speaking to Balaam
7. confusion of languages at Babel
8. Moses's (or Aaron's) rod changed into a serpent
9. Daniel delivered from the lions' den
10. rain in answer to Elijah's prayer
11. plague of darkness over the land of Egypt
12. parting of the Red Sea
13. water gushing forth from a rock when struck by Moses
14. the great flood of Noah
15. the fall of the walls of Jericho
16. Jonah and the great fish
17. Aaron's rod blossoming
18. dew on Gideon's fleece
19. shadow returning on the sundial at the word of Isaiah
20. sun standing still at the time of Joshua

Glimpsing the Gospels:

1. Gabriel
2. Simeon
3. Egypt
4. The feeding of the five thousand

5. As soon as Jesus entered the boat, it immediately appeared at the land where the disciples were going.
6. Simon
7. The rich, young ruler
8. He had only a linen cloth over his body. When seized, he ran off naked.
9. Cleopas was one of the two people Jesus appeared to on the road to Emmaus.
10. Jesus breathed on them, that they would receive the Holy Spirit.

This Is Your Mission:

1. Miletus
2. Antioch
3. Thessalonica
4. Asia
5. Philippi
6. Iconium
7. Corinth
8. Caesarea
9. Derbe
10. Lystra
11. Jerusalem
12. Troas
13. Ephesus
14. Perga
15. Athens
16. Berea
17. Cyprus

All about Paul:

1. T
2. F
3. T

4. T
5. F
6. F
7. F
8. T
9. F
10. T
11. T
12. F
13. T
14. T
15. F
16. T
17. T
18. F
19. T
20. T

Exhortation Exercise:

1. Rejoice evermore.
2. Despise not prophesyings.
3. Pray without ceasing.
4. Quench not the Spirit.
5. Abstain from all appearance of evil.
6. Prove all things; hold fast that which is good.
7. In everything give thanks, for this is the will of God in Christ Jesus concerning you.

It's a Miracle:

1. walking on the sea
2. fig tree withered
3. two blind men cured
4. woman with issue of blood healed

5. catch (draught) of fish
6. water made wine

The New Jerusalem:

Move backward four letters in the alphabet to decode the letters.

1. water of life
2. new heaven and new earth
3. light
4. twelve gates of pearl
5. throne of God
6. streets of gold
7. no night
8. tree of life
9. no more death
10. precious stones

Promises for You:

1. Confess our sins
2. Judge not
3. Give
4. Trust and delight in the Lord
5. Delight in God's Word and meditate on it
6. Trust in the lord, lean not on our own understanding, and acknowledge Him in everything
7. Confess Jesus before men
8. Abide in Christ, and his words abide in us
9. Trust in God and keep our minds set on Him
10. Put on the whole armor of God
11. Submit ourselves to God and resist the devil

12. Walk in the Spirit
13. Cast our burdens on the lord
14. Continue in well doing without growing weary or giving up
15. Continue in faith and patience

Just Like Jesus:

1. acceptable
2. bold
3. clean
4. devout
5. edifying
6. faithful
7. gentle
8. humble
9. incorruptible
10. joyful
11. kind
12. lovely
13. mindful
14. noble
15. obedient
16. pure
17. quiet
18. righteous
19. steadfast
20. true
21. undefiled
22. vigilant
23. whole
24. yielded
25. zealous

"Be Attitudes":

Beatitude:

1. poor in spirit
2. mourn
3. meek
4. pure in heart
5. persecuted for righteousness sake
6. merciful
7. hunger and thirst after righteousness
8. peacemakers

Promise:

A. see God
B. inherit the earth
C. kingdom of heaven
D. obtain mercy
E. be comforted
F. called the children of God
G. be filled
1-C
2-E
3-B
4-A
5-C
6-D
7-G
8-F

Parable Puzzle:

1. unjust judge
2. wicked husbandmen
3. talents
4. pearl of great price
5. fig tree
6. ten virgins
7. house built upon the rock
8. leaven
9. wheat and tares
10. prodigal son
11. laborers in the vineyard
12. lost coin
13. Good Samaritan
14. lost sheep
15. sower

Fellow Believers:

1. Matthias
2. Aquila
3. Agabus
4. Mary
5. Onesimus
6. Barnabas
7. Cornelius
8. Stephen
9. Timothy
10. Apollos
11. Epaphroditus
12. Phoebe
13. Silas
14. Theophilus
15. Dorcus

Famous Pray-ers:

1. N
2. B
3. F
4. H
5. O
6. D
7. A
8. K
9. E
10. L
11. M
12. G
13. J
14. I
15. C

Precious Gems: Put the kingdom of God first.

Most Unusual—But True:

1. locusts, honey
2. fifteen
3. axe head
4. sun
5. six, six
6. stone
7. viper
8. dead (dry) bones
9. bed
10. Solomon
11. Isaiah
12. shave

13. left-handed
14. backward
15. Moses

Work for the Lord:

1. baker
2. farmer
3. servant
4. architect
5. educator
6. newspaperman
7. astronomer
8. geologist
9. soldier
10. banker
11. statesman
12. doctor
13. builder
14. jeweler
15. carpenter
16. lawyer
17. florist
18. ambassador
19. musician
20. philosopher

Famous Bible Women:

1. Leah-i
2. Tamar-a
3. Vashti-k
4. Deborah-b
5. Mary-j
6. Rachel-l

7. Rebekah-h
8. Michal-g
9. Elizabeth-d
10. Serah-f
11. Tabitha-c
12. Ruth-e

Bible Numbers Quiz:

1. 969
2. 153
3. 12
4. 1000
5. 5000
6. 40, 40
7. 7
8. 120
9. 666
10. 285,000
11. 88
12. 300
13. 24
14. 144,000
15. 12

First Things:

1. C
2. A
3. C
4. D
5. B
6. D

7. A
8. C
9. B
10. D
11. B
12. A

Animal Backers:

1. ox
2. dog
3. eagles
4. leopard
5. calves
6. sheep, wolves
7. serpents, doves
8. camel
9. goats
10. fox
11. lamb
12. lion
13. horses

Insect Inspection:

Across: caterpillar, moth, grasshopper, fly, flea, earthworm, lice, spider

Down: locust, ant, beetle, gnat

Diagonal: bee, hornet

Letters spelled out: Not a one could be found

Name That Mountain:

1. F
2. H
3. C
4. I
5. B
6. A
7. G
8. J
9. E
10. D

Tree Stumpers:

Across: cedar, fir, elm. willow, sycamore, cypress

Down: chestnut, myrtle, fig, palm, olive, pomegranate

Diagonal: poplar, pine, oak

Printed in the United States
by Baker & Taylor Publisher Services